SIX CATALAN POETS

SIX
CATALAN
POETS

Translated by
Anna Crowe

Edited and introduced by
Pere Ballart

PUBLICATIONS
2013

Published by Arc Publications
Nanholme Mill, Shaw Wood Road
Todmorden, OL14 6DA, UK
www.arcpublications.co.uk

ISBN: 978 1906570 60 6

The publishers are grateful to the authors and,
in the case of previously published works, to their publishers
for allowing their poems to be included in this anthology.

Cover image: 'Hemograma: RL 2-10-98' (1998)
(blood on slide, projected onto photographic paper)
by Joan Fontcuberta

The translation of this work was supported
by a grant from the Institut Ramon Llull

**LLLL institut
ramon llull**
Catalan Language and Culture

The 'New Voices from Europe and Beyond' anthology series
is published in co-operation with Literature Across Frontiers
which receives support from the
Culture Programme of the EU.

LITERATURE
ACROSS
FRONTIERS

**Arc Publications 'New Voices from Europe and Beyond'
Series Editor: Alexandra Büchler**

CONTENTS

Six Catalan Poets is the ninth volume in a series of bilingual anthologies which brings contemporary poetry from around Europe to English-language readers. It is not by accident that the tired old phrase about poetry being 'lost in translation' came out of an English-speaking environment, out of a tradition that has always felt remarkably uneasy about translation – of contemporary works, if not the classics. Yet poetry can be and *is* 'found' in translation; in fact, any good translation *reinvents* the poetry of the original, and we should always be aware that any translation is the outcome of a dialogue between two cultures, languages and different poetic sensibilities, between collective as well as individual imaginations, conducted by two voices, that of the poet and of the translator, and joined by a third interlocutor in the process of reading.

And it is this dialogue that is so important to writers in countries and regions where translation has always been an integral part of the literary environment and has played a role in the development of local literary tradition and poetics. Writing without reading poetry from many different traditions would be unthinkable for the poets in the anthologies of this series, many of whom are accomplished translators who consider poetry in translation to be part of their own literary background and an important source of inspiration.

While the series 'New Voices from Europe and Beyond' aims to keep a finger on the pulse of the here-and-now of international poetry by presenting the work of a small number of contemporary poets, each collection, edited by a guest editor, has its own focus and rationale for the selection of the poets and poems. In this anthology, readers meet six poets writing in a language with a long literary tradition and a modern history of struggle for its retrieval, recognition and autonomy. Catalan literature has had to assert itself vigorously to be recognized and appreciated as part of the vibrant, autonomous culture whose artists had long before conquered the international scene. The poets presented here belong to a generation born in the 60s and 70s, that has benefited from and actively participated in the period of reassertion of Catalan culture made possible by successive political steps towards ever greater autonomy, not only though their writing but also though their work in the cultural and academic sphere. Their poetry, characterized by intellectual rigour and artistic awareness heightened by the need to continuously re-examine one's position in multiple cultural and linguistic frameworks, is contextualized in the editor's informative and comprehensive introduction and superbly rendered in translations specially commissioned for this collection.

My thanks go to everyone who made this edition possible.
Alexandra Büchler

A (TELESCOPIC) LOOK AT CATALAN POETRY

In 2003, Arthur Terry's excellent *A Companion to Catalan Literature* opened with the avowed purpose of shedding light for the benefit of the English-speaking reader on "an important but, on the whole neglected, area of Peninsular culture". Terry states that during the past century Catalan writers have been far less well-known outside their own country than artists from other disciplines, such as Gaudí, Miró, Tàpies, Pau Casals, Montserrat Caballé, whereas all have exhibited "a similar degree of excellence".[1] Ten years later, the situation has barely changed: the literature of the main territories in which Catalan is spoken (Catalonia, Valencia and the Balearic Islands)[2] still fails to compete with the cultural (and touristic) attraction of its respective capitals, Barcelona in particular. Furthermore, given its political dependence, it has to compete while always being associated, in one way or another, with the majority culture and language of the State to which these territories, administratively speaking, belong: Spain and Castilian. This is a shocking situation when we realise that we are speaking about a thousand-year-old literature whose earliest manifestations date from the twelfth century, written in a language spoken by ten million people (the twelfth most spoken language of Europe) and with in excess of ten thousand titles published each year, especially in Barcelona, an important publishing centre. With the Franco dictatorship over and after more than thirty years of democracy, the country retains intact its unfulfilled national aspirations which would, given the opportunity, bring together all aspects of its culture. Meanwhile, we have had to wait for occasions such as the Frankfurt Book Fair of 2007, in which Catalan culture was special guest, in order to reveal its quantity and excellence to the outside world. I would like to think, as the anthologist of these six Catalan poets, that their publication is one more step and, I hope, a firm one, in this direction. After all, we should have confidence in the future, first because literary activity, fed by new recruits, never ceases throughout the Catalan countries, and secondly because history shows, every step of the way, how our culture has been strong enough to overcome critical situations far more adverse than the present. It will be useful to cast our minds back.

In 1953, one of the most clear-sighted Catalan poets of the twentieth century, Gabriel Ferrater, published in the Spanish magazine *Ínsula* a grim diagnosis of the health of Catalan culture: 'Madame se meurt' (The Lady is Dying).[3] Ferrater was alluding to the lecture given by the French poet, Paul Valéry, in

Barcelona in 1924, with its serious warning to the local intelligentsia that it should devote itself above all to prose: the author of *Le Cimetière Marin* was flagging up the example of another minority culture that has become extinct, Occitan, which, even when represented by figures like the Nobel prizewinner, Frédéric Mistral, was already "dead through having been nothing but poetry". Ferrater used the argument to warn how Catalan culture too was in grave danger, in spite of producing a rich flow of poetry. His fear was that without powerful prose and within the frame of a life "void of legalities" – it is easy to see here a denunciation of the Franco regime's persecution of Catalan language and identity – the Catalan people would one day end by adopting, as an instrument of expression, a language other than their own. More than half a century later, Catalan has not been replaced, but has been forced to carry on side by side with Castilian. It may seem that Ferrater, bird of ill omen, was exaggerating, but an historical overview of Catalan poetry, full of brilliance and shadows, is enough to make clear the real perils that this writer was alerting us to.

As heir to the Provençal troubadour tradition, poetry in Catalan knew a moment of extraordinary splendour in the fifteenth century when, under the influence of Petrarch, it included the giant figure of Ausiàs March, the most prodigious lyric poet among the many others flourishing at that time, and an example of meditative introspection. But it is equally true that, a little later, it had to overcome a dense silence that lasted from the sixteenth to the eighteenth centuries: the so-called 'Decadence', a period of Spanish political and cultural hegemony during which this illustrious tradition seemed to be alive only in the weak, anonymous beat of popular poetry. Without the impetus, Romantic in origin, associated with a renewed national consciousness that animated what became known in the nineteenth century as the 'Renaissance', the future of poetry and indeed of Catalan culture as a whole would have been disastrous. The country recovered confidence in its language through poetry that was epic in concept and patriotic in tone, and it would not be wrong to see its history from then on as a slow recovery towards catching up with Western poetry after three centuries of abeyance. From this time of re-establishment then, the principal names within the genre are those who were most responsible for reducing that *décalage*: Jacint Verdaguer (1845-1902), energetic forger of a poetic language; Joan Maragall (1860-1911), an example of moral sincerity; and Josep Carner (1884-1970), a believer in the perfect form, though not as an obstacle to the communication of deeply held feelings, but rather as their best ally. In the course of his work we witness, as though in a speeded-up film, the irreversible awakening of the Catalan poetic. From the beginning of the twentieth century, with the language now become a trustworthy and standardized instrument, until the fracture imposed by the Civil War, the authentic flourishing of the genre produced a handful of first class writers: Carles Riba, J. V. Foix, Joan Salvat-Papasseit, Joan Oliver / Pere Quart, and Agustí Bartra. Taken together, they covered to an extraordinary degree the whole gamut of forms, themes and tones, from rationalist abstraction to surrealism, from eroticism to satire, from the hymn to the elegy. The diaspora of exile, the harsh Francoist repression and the premature disappearance of writers such as Bartomeu Rosselló-Pòrcel and Màrius Torres, gave rise to fears of another period of obscurity, and nothing could better exemplify this than the death of Carles Riba – becoming the most powerful symbol of cultural resistance – in 1959. The end of the fifties seemed to presage a definite decline; fortunately, however, the reasons for despondency soon proved to be without foundation.

In fact the following decade could not have begun in more promising fashion. The appearance in 1960 of *Da nuces pueris* (Give the Children Nuts to Eat) by Gabriel Ferrater (1922-1972) and *La pell de brau* (The Bull's Hide) by Salvador Espriu (1913-1985) attest to the widespread evidence of an engaged civil realism, but which each poet understands in his own way. Espriu oriented his usual meditation on death towards historic circumstances; Ferrater, on the other hand, launched a poetry of moral experience (in the style of poets like Auden or Graves) which his later work, collected in 1968 as *Les dones i els dies*, was to make yet more dense and subtle (translated into English in 2004, it aroused, for example, the admiration of Seamus Heaney).[4] The influence in Catalonia of these two great poets is similar to that which made Blai Bonet (1926-1997) the great reviver of Balearic poetry and Vicent Andrés Estellés (1924-1993) the Valencian poet of greatest importance after Ausiàs March. This decade finally also brought to fruition three bodies of work as notable as they are distinctive: the tireless experimentalism of Joan Brossa (1919-1998), the figurative symbolism of Joan Vinyoli (1919-1984), and the profound and pared-down diction of Miquel Martí i Pol (1929-2003), whose popularity gave him, right up until his death, the prominence reserved for a national poet.

The following decade, that of the seventies, is one of slow political transition to democracy. It is a time when the exponents of either meditative, confessional and autobiographical realism, or experimentalism, or concrete poetry, consolidate their positions. In the first group are those who offer a moral, critical poetry, which bears down on the past and on memory: a poetry of experience or rather of 'inexperience' which each individual comes up against when constructing their personality.[5] Here we should include, in chronological order, Joan Margarit (born 1938), author of a copious series of titles, of which those published in the nineties (*Edat roja, Els motius del llop, Aiguaforts* – Red Age, The Motives of the Wolf, Etchings) are the ones that illustrate his style most clearly. Successor in popular acclaim to Martí i Pol, Margarit is a poet of emotive power, whose tone is increasingly trenchant and austere. Marta Pessarrodona (born 1941) composes learned, civilised poems and always in the form of a confiding conversation, as a defence against time and the threats posed by history, in that her writing weighs the personal as much as the collective, from *Setembre 30* (September 30, 1969) to *Animals i plantes* (Animals and Plants, 2010). Narcís Comadira (born 1942), with a feeling for language akin to Carner, is always elegant and plastic (as he is in his other art, painting) and has created out of personal experience highly flexible poetic material: *Formes de l'ombra* (Shadow Shapes, 2002) gathers together almost forty years of sustained production. With its precocious exploration of beat poetry, the work of Francesc Parcerisas (born 1944) is the paradigm of poetry rooted in experience, beginning with the huge success of *L'edat d'or* (The Golden Age, 1983), whose title is suggestive of a perfect balance between sensuality and rationalism which his subsequent collections have made more profound and expressionistic. Two other poets of this period deserving of attention are Pere Rovira (born 1947) in whom the themes of love and death take on Baudelairean overtones, and Àlex Susanna (born 1957), active promoter of things cultural, whose poetry is remarkable for its desire to construct "verbal models of private life", as urged by Spender.

Champions of a less narrative lyric, other poets have taken a more experimental route. Among the more avant-guarde is Enric Casasses (born 1951), a frequent performer at recitals and readings. Transgressing and naif, meticulously crafted and dadaist, the outstanding collections of his poetic corpus are *La cosa aquella* (That Thing, 1992), *Calç* (Lime, 1996) and *Que dormim?* (You Think We Should Sleep?, 2002). When considering poetry that raises questions about the limits of language, we should mention the work of Pere Gimferrer (born 1945) who straddles the Castilian and Catalan traditions. Books that stand out among his Catalan collections are *Els miralls* (Mirrors, 1970), *L'espai desert* (The

Empty Space, 1977) and *El vendaval* (The Hurricane, 1988), char-
acterized by rich, intellectually complex and elliptical writing.
The work of Maria Mercè Marçal (1952-1998) sets down a marker
for the consistency of her voice as a woman. The experience of
the femininine, motherhood, and illness forms the basis of her
books, *Sal Oberta* (Bare-faced Salt, 1982), *La germana, l'estrangera*
(Sister, Stranger, 1985), *Desglaç* (Thaw, 1989) or the posthumous
Raó del cos (The Body's Reason, 2000). And it would not be right
to disregard other voices from a period of vigorous activity in
the Balearics and in Valencia: Miquel Àngel Riera, Bartomeu
Fiol, Miquel Bauçà and Ponç Pons in the islands, and Josep Piera,
Marc Granell and Enric Sòria from the Valencian area.

It has become famous, that passage in *Flaubert's Parrot* where
Julian Barnes says that "the past is a distant, receding coastline,
and we are all in the same boat", from which we gaze at the land
through "a set of telescopes". Certainly, the closer we are to what
we are looking at, the more scruples we have when the moment
comes to describe and sum it up; whereas things that are a long
way off we can dispatch quite happily with a single phrase. In
my exposé, (which has obviously gone on lengthening the closer
I have come to the present) I have now reached the decades of the
eighties and nineties, which are those in which the older poets of
this anthology began to publish and to acquire their reputations.
It will be simpler, therefore, for me to speak about this period by
concentrating on the poets I have chosen, whose skilful and di-
verse character seems to me to represent the multi-faceted nature
of recent Catalan poetry. One thing is clear: Ferrater's prophecy,
happily, has not yet been fulfilled: "Madame" is alive and well,
and poetry in our language aspires to being taken for granted as
a normal phenomenon, just as it is in any other country.

Six (Possible) Catalan Poets

Tracing a map of Catalan poetry of recent years is a difficult
task since no summary can do justice to the diversity of styles
that co-exist in published collections, journals and public read-
ings, all of which include not only the poets of recent generations
but also the older ones, whose longevity and energy mean that
they are still present, simultaneously, alongside younger voices,
often acting as their mentors. In countries where everyone obeys
the same aesthetic dictat it must be easy enough to assemble a
composite picture and to detail the small variants: in Catalonia,
Valencia and Mallorca, however, there are so many actively-writ-
ing poets and with such divergent agendas that any synthesis

is impossible. Today, the close proximity in time and space of, for example, extraordinary adventures such as the experimental exercises by Victor Sunyol (born 1955), the dense and exquisite symbolism of Susanna Rafart (born 1962), the Mallarmean work of Albert Roig (born 1959) or the daring and critical constructions of Sebastià Alzamora (born 1972), to name but a few (and any of the previously mentioned still writing), is proof enough, in spite of the fine prose being written here – Valéry was listened to in the end – that Catalonia is above all a land of poets; and, it should be added, of poets who are very jealous of their creative independence. Having to choose, therefore, only six to be at once representative, varied and of the first water, constituted, because of excess and not because of any defect, an authentic *embarras de choix*. My final option was to choose six poets, five men and one woman: four Catalans, one Valencian and one Mallorcan, who were born between 1963 and 1972 and who, although they lived through the tail end of the dictatorship, had been formed under a democratic regime. Taken together, their work could not be more modern, comprehensive or polyphonic: in the writing of all six, the reader will find politics and history cohabiting with the intimate experience of love (both heterosexual and homo-erotic), learned allusion and popular image, stanzaic rigour and freedom of form, the song to the land of one's birth and hymn to the voyage, doubt over the expressive possibilities of language together with pride in the blazing word fuelled by enthusiasm or by anger. The reader will judge to what point they share, as I think, the secrets of the self-same art, and at the same time to what point they are singular and unique. Let us look at them, then, one by one.

CARLES TORNER (born Barcelona, 1963) is an outstanding exponent of poetic engagement against inequality and political violence. Written when he was only twenty, his first books, *A la ciutat blanca* (In the White City, 1984) and *Als límits de la sal* (On the Frontiers of Salt, 1985) already reveal a predilection for the formal side of his craft, with the poetry of J. V. Foix as model, a fact that explains his preference for strict forms such as the sonnet and for a concision of expression and a liking for archaisms – see 'Let Us Think Death' (p. 29). Coinciding in time with Torner's aligning and afiliating himself with cultural initiatives such as the secretariat of Catalan PEN or the NGO in support of the Universal Declaration of Linguistic Rights, his collection, *L'àngel del saqueig* (The Plundering Angel, 1989) also marked a change in his writing, now completely devoted to building a sensibility alert always to the "piercing pain / on the altar of memory", which is a consequence of the injustice of the world ('The Plundering Angel', p. 29). The poet is in the final analysis attentive to the cries of those who suffer, whether of the "child weeping" here and now, at home ('The Child', p. 29), or of the victims of the Balkans War, an armed conflict that would determine the conception of his next book, *Viure després* (Living Afterwards, 1998), in which the poet has learned that, like Zacharias in the New Testament, he is called to serve the voice he has recovered in order to spread his message. If this collection was triggered by the disasters of Vukovar and Srebrenica, the next book was born out of indignation over the brutal political assassination in 2006 of the Russian journalist, Anna Politkovskaya. *La núvia d'Europa* (The Bride of Europe, 2008) echoes with the conflicts that shake the planet and destroy the freedom of individuals and peoples, and Torner forges his poetry into a testimony that is at once memorial and denunciation. The poem 'Untranslating Europe' (p. 41) is the cornerstone; a *tour de force* in which lines by the Polish poet Adam Zagajewski bring the poetic voice to an intense reflection on linguistic diversity and cultural and historical frontiers. His undisguisedly religious humanism on the one hand, and a tireless solidarity with the humiliated and wronged on the other, mean that he is close to predecessors such as Verdaguer or Salvat-Papasseit, and makes logical the presence of Biblical motifs with rebellious proclamations, under such unequivocal banners as "in the face of fear, the only truth's a scream" ('Device', p. 35). Given the mingling of ethical conscience and emotion, it is no surprise to find that one of his finest registers is the elegiac, as exemplified in a deeply moving poem like 'The Red Van' (p. 37), written in memory of the Jewish poet, Yael Langella.

GEMMA GORGA (born Barcelona, 1968) once said that she demanded from poetry "a mixture of emotion and wonder" and that is exactly what readers receive from her four collections published to date – *Ocellania* (1997), *El desordre de les mans* (The Hands' Disorder, 2003), *Instruments òptics* (Optical Instruments, 2005) and *Llibre dels minuts* (Book of Minutes, 2006). Emotion is furnished by a constant and explicit use of the second person singular, the 'tu', the familiarity of the frame of the poem's experience and an imagining that often has recourse to childish and domestic symbols. Wonder, on the other hand, stems from the extraordinary, microscopic attention the poet gives to objects and details. Out of these modest, everyday things poetic situations are composed which then become a suitable vehicle for the poet's fears and longings (Gorga poeticises everything, often on a precarious base of feelings), thus distancing them from the poet's "I". Her long, figurative verse-form, which can often evoke the poems of Francesc Parcerisas, has given way in her most recent collection, *Llibre dels minuts* to a highly successful experiment in the field of the prose poem. But whatever form it is presented in, what immediately captivates in Gorga's poetry is the almost hypnotic atmosphere that her exercises in introspection manage to create. Experience, always intimate – we could not find a voice that is further from what is usually known as civic poetry – here appears stripped of all superfluous information and pulls us along with a certain feeling of unease, aroused by the continual switching between literal and metaphorical meanings, towards sometimes terrible conclusions ('Stones', p. 61, and 'Rest', p. 65) but which are always expressed in a serene and immutably placid tone of voice. In the same way, the poet appears able to confront the most serious metaphysical problems with the innocence of one who has enough of that quality to be able to use a handful of simple images and familiar actions, a quality which her most recent prose poems seem to accentuate further. It is also clear that there runs through her work a constant, resigned preoccupation with the limits of language and the arbitrariness of the symbols of which it is composed: "you'll never be able to discover what each thing is beyond the tired meaning in the dictionary", she says in one of her most recent compositions, and this statement seems to recall one where Wittgenstein relativized the capacity of the word 'pain' to designate precisely this concept. And in fact Parcerisas, who wrote the introduction to her *El desordre de les mans*, detects in Gorga's voice the accent of "someone who is ready to overcome with bitter irony any contradiction or adversity".

Anyone who does not know him will perhaps associate MANUEL FORCANO (born Barcelona, 1968) with the ideas of the poetic group to which he once belonged, the so-called *imparables* (unstoppables), and that may give rise to confusion about his style.[6] The truth is that, far from belonging to the iconoclasm of that group, Forcano has in fact always written evocative lyrics, full of delicacy and sensibility, from his earliest collections, *Les mans descalces* (Barefoot Hands, 1993) and *D'un record a l'altre* (From One Memory to the Next, 1993); as opposed to the philosophy of the 'unstoppables', which is primarily antisentimental, it can be said of his work that he has ended by becoming our foremost love-poet. The pure expression of desire, of admiration for physical beauty, finds in his writing a perfect gloss, in the style of Cavafy, in characters and episodes of ancient history. With the consolidation of his work (with *De nit* [By Night, 1999]; *Corint*

[Corinth, 2000]; *Com un persa* [Like a Persian, 2001]; and *El tren de Bagdad* [The Bagdhad Train, 2004]), his poems, beautiful with spaces and images, have opened up more and more to the landscape and peoples of the Middle East: this setting is well-suited to their lyrical character through its southern sensuality and because it has always been historically an area of contact between cultures and civilizations. Traveller and great connoisseur of the Semitic world, the poet proved in 2008 with his collection, *Llei d'estrangeria* (Law Governing Aliens) and with his latest book *Estàtues sense cap* (Headless Statues) that these subjects attract him, not because they are exotic or decorative, but because they allow him to unite the autobiographical element of his poetry with a meditation on ethnic and cultural otherness. From the stylistic point of view, they are compositions which successfully avoid the inherent risk in making love their almost single theme. The conviction with which Forcano has always handled the device of the simile ("My love is / like a plane's white trail in the sky...", p. 85) is the guarantee that the poem, whose simplicity never strays far from the anecdotal, will present itself to its readers as a supremely imaginative invitation. The author's philosophy (see 'Poètica' [Poetics], from his book *Com un persa*) is that of one who knows that memory preserves only a feeble trace of pleasurable experiences, and that for that reason one must hedonistically seek to multiply them. The poem thus becomes a dazzling register of instants of plenitude or of moments, as in the magnificent 'At the Café Sahel in Aleppo' (p. 97), from the string of episodes in a love affair. His talent for avoiding any monotony shapes itself in metaphors that are ever more rich and various and, on occasion, as in the poem 'Walking through the Call' (p. 107), in a complex weaving together of the poem's moral tensions.

It is highly significant that between the first collection by the poet JOSEP LLUÍS AGUILÓ (born Portocristo, Mallorca, 1967) and the rest of his work there is a gap of eighteen years: stretching from the adolescent *Cants d'Arjau* (Songs from the Helm, 1986), to the group of his four mature collections, the earliest published in 2004, this is in reality the thoughtful building of a solid literary project, which retains from that first title (see 'XII "The calm of dusk...",, p. 113) only a permanent liking for mythological allusions. Indeed, the sequence formed by *La biblioteca secreta* (The Secret Library) and *L'estació de les ombres* (The Season of Shadows, 2004), *Monstres* (Monsters, 2005) and *Llunari* (Lunar, 2008) embraces a kaleidoscopic poetic adventure, that is culturalist in its symbols and in complete harmony with the eclecticism with which postmodernism juxtaposes the most learned and the most popular icons. In Aguiló's poetry, therefore, we find coexisting happily traditional *rondeaux* and the most bookish myths, Minotaur and Flying Dutchman hand in hand with fairytale, rustic representations of the devil ('The Devil's Bridges', p. 115, and Medusa rubbing shoulders with the heroes of the far west ('Tumbleweed', p. 129). They are, therefore, books rich in experience and memories, but above all – in their painstaking architecture – rich in correspondences: the variegated, polychromatic cast of literary and mythic characters whom Aguiló conjures up in poem after poem are, by analogy, as the critic Damià Pons has remarked, "a web of experiences, feelings, expectations or fears that are in reality inherent to the human condition down the ages". The poet sees clearly that literary fictions are the only way out when life confronts us with its adverse side ('The Attic', p. 123) and that the writing of poetry is a process as laborious as it is absorbing ('Words', p. 121; 'I Have Lost a Few Lines', p. 127). One of the most characteristic features of his style is that he never explores any universal aspect of the human condition without illustrating it profusely with a wealth of images and finely-drawn, detailed historical accounts ('Parallelisms', p. 115 and 'The Contract', p. 133). His latest volume, *Llunari*, takes up once more the theme of the uncertainty of life, and in looking for omens capable of explanation it has recourse to elements of fantasy (labyrinths, hells, guardians, palaces with golden pillars, apocalypses), which the poet reveals again as allegories of our everyday universe. This imagery and the play of voices deployed in all his books – from the artifice of pronouns to the frequent use of the dramatic monologue – mean that when the time comes to define Aguiló's lyric world, one is irresistibly reminded of the work of Jorge Luís Borges.

ELIES BARBERÀ (born Xàtiva, València, 1970) writes poetry on which chaotic, urban experience leaves a profound and disturbing mark, as his collection *Allà on les grues nien* (Where the Cranes Nest, 2009) shows. The deep-rooted Western tradition of disaffection for the city, from Baudelaire and Verhaeren to Apollinaire, or from Eliot to Lorca, finds a critical echo here: the poet mingles defamiliarizing description with the adoption of a prophetic, oracular tone that conjures up the evils of a civilization of plastic and security cameras, imprisoned in concrete. In total contrast to this panorama, there is the edenic vision that memory retains of village life, the idealizing of kindly, family relationships that are human-scale (the theme that runs right through *Aixàtiva, Aixàtiva* [Ah, Xàtiva, Xàtiva, 2008], and present here in the lovely poem 'Earliest Smell', p. 147). Equally adept at writing metrical verse or prose poems, Barberà is impelled to write night-walking poems whose irony is directed at the self, or to melancholic epiphanies, or to long tirades against the thousand faces of the dehumanized city, in the form of counter-ode or sarcastic 'post-card' in prose. His style is characterized by making lists, enumerating, rushing headlong, and by an obsession with lowercase writing that reserves capital letters for large concepts such as Order, or Conscience, or City. Nevertheless, the visceral nature of his diction or his images (*Ulls, budells, cor* [Eyes, Bowels, Heart, 2012] is the title he gave to a recent collection) never conceals his recondite nostalgia for a more authentic life, accessible only through sweetened memory, evasive fantasies or alcoholic fictions. Surely, however, the aspect of his style that most fascinates the reader is the dexterity with which Barberà moves, chameleon-like, between four very different kinds of poem, all of them represented in this anthology: the transgressive event, such as imagining Mickey Mouse drunk, the victim of the American Dream ('Unlucky Mickey Mouse', p. 139), or Jesus Christ acclaimed by the masses only when dressed as a footballer, as though he were Leo Messi ('Ashes to Ashes', p. 147); the lofty poem with its learned allusions and serious reflections ('Oratory' p. 145); the generational and autobiographical portrait ('The Coward's Hymn', p. 141; or '20 November 75, Day of Ponds', p. 149), which remembers the day of Franco's death seen through the eyes of the child the poet was then; or finally, the most characteristic example from his latest collection, *Allà on les grues nien*, a satire on postindustrial society, with a nod to Swift or Huxley, which demonstrates how everything in the city is fake and made of plastic: in flagrant contradiction, the well-to-do adolescent kills herself, anorexic, dying of hunger, while the homeless man is the archaeologist of the refuse-containers ('Sister Anorexia', p. 153; 'Archaeologist', p. 153).

The poetry of JORDI JULIÀ (born Sant Celoni, Barcelona, 1972) encourages us to remember that nowadays, as T. S. Eliot notes, lyric poetry is not defined by the expression of personality but its evasion. Julià belongs to that tradition of poets who are happy to speak about themselves, but assume that the reader will only be able to share those experiences that are based on a well-defined anecdote and in a voice whose tone and nuances are true to life. His lyric works, up to the present day, from *Els grills que no he matat* (The Crickets I Haven't Killed, 1998), comprise fifteen titles, which constitute a particular style in alternating two kinds of book: in the first, in an exercise in ventriloquism unusual in the Catalan tradition, the poet, transformed into editor, translator,

or anthologist, has managed to invoke the most diverse aliases –
such as the would-be North American lyrics of *Un lleu plugim* (A
Gentle Rain, 2009) or the poet Alexandra March of *Hiverns suaus*
(Mild Winters, 2005), whom one critic, unaware of the device,
hailed as a promising new voice in women's writing in Cata-
lan. The second 'manner', from *Tornar el dilluns* (Going Home on
Monday, 2002), *Murs de contenció* (Walls of Contention, 2004) and
Els déus de fang (The Gods of Mud, 2007), concerns itself with an
objective account of "the moral life" of the first-person speaker
in the poem – the poetic 'I' – and its most characteristic features:
formal expertise, the narrative concept of the poem – with a pen-
chant for the animal fable – the use of the objective correlative
and an always imaginative blending of the long poem and the
dramatic monologue. *Principi de plaer* (The Pleasure Principle,
2007) and *Planisferi lunar* (Lunar Planisphere, 2008), the most
rounded of his books, combine an appraisal of the fluidity of
postmodern society with an elegy for the changes in a personal
world which threaten the very identity of the I. What stands out
as going hand in hand with this is the author's own formulation
of theory: in his essay *Modernitat del món fungible* (Modernity of
the Replaceable World, 2006) he uses the oblique term, "reflexive
realism", to describe the poetry of his generation. The antholo-
gized poems, such as 'Glances' (with its meaningful allusion to
Norman Rockwell in the epigraph, p. 165), embody a benevolent
desire to tell stories about anonymous people ('Saturday Men',
p. 167; 'The Forbidden City', p. 169). Poems like 'Bad Readers'
(p. 171), 'Tortoises' (p. 175), and 'The Hidden Bird' (p. 183) make
clever use of the analogy which, with deliberately varied metre,
embraces both the social conventions of the public world ('The
Pleasure Principle', p. 175) and a retreat into a personal landscape
which progress is on the way to erasing ('Looking for Roots', p.
181). In his finest poems, such as 'Deep in the Flesh' (p. 179), or
'Older Cousins' (p. 181), for example, Julià exhibits the narrative
power and depth of moral analysis which in his own tradition he
has found in Gabriel Ferrater and, in other literatures, in poets
such as Robert Frost or Cesare Pavese.

One of the finest Catalan essayists of the twentieth century,
the Valencian, Joan Fuster, concludes his *Literatura catalana con-
temporània* (1971) by recalling that "in a literature such as Cata-
lan, whose history is a struggle for survival, and for 'material'
survival, one cannot avoid speaking with a deal of passion and,
therefore, with much implicit trust". This anthology would like
to make that passion its own and to succeed in bringing it to the
maximum number of readers: at bottom, on that implicit trust

also depends the hope – and it is a hope that the six poets anthologized here, and I myself, all share – that Catalan and its literature will continue to survive for many years.

Pere Ballart

NOTES

[1] Arthur Terry, *A Companion to Catalan Literature* (Woodbridge: Tamesis), 2003, pp. vii-viii. The much-missed critic from York, who died in 2004, has been the best ambassador for Catalan literature in the Anglo-Saxon world. I would like these pages to be a modest but grateful tribute to his memory.

[2] I refer only to those that lie within the Spanish State, but Catalan is also spoken in Andorra, the Roussillon (France) and in the Alguer (Sardinia, Italy), so that there are altogether four states that share its linguistic area.

[3] Gabriel Ferrater, "Madame se meurt...", *Sobre literatura. Assaigs, articles i altres textos. 1951-71*, edited by Joan Ferraté (Barcelona: Edicions 62, 1979), pp. 81-88.

[4] Gabriel Ferrater, *Women and Days*, trans. Arthur Terry (Todmorden: Arc Publications, 2004).

[5] The English reader has the opportunity of reading some of all these poets in translation in their own language. For example, Joan Margarit, *Tugs in the fog* (Bloodaxe Books, 2006), and *Strangely Happy* (Bloodaxe Books, 2010) (both translated by Anna Crowe); Marta Pessarrodona, *Confession* (Poetry Ireland / Tyrone Guthrie Centre, 1998); Francesc Parcerisas, *The Golden Age and Other Poems*, trans. Sam Abrams (Barcelona: Institute of North American Studies, 1992); or the anthology (also translated by Sam Abrams) *Comadira, Gimferrer, Margarit, Parcerisas, Pessarrodona: Five Poets* (Barcelona: Institute of North American Studies, 1988).

[6] *Imparables* (Unstoppables) is the name of a poetry anthology published in 2004 by Proa, edited by the critics Sam Abrams and Francesco Ardolino, which showcased a group of new poets, born between 1962 and 1972. Its main nucleus, united more by personal friendship than by any obvious stylistic identity, included, as well as Manuel Forcano, the poets Sebastià Alzamora (1972) and Hèctor Bofill (1973). The arguable cohesion of the group and the real disparity in their aesthetics have with time, and in spite of the very likeable quality of some of the participants, weakened an initiative that made a loud but highly opportunistic appearance, and whose character was eminently the brainchild of its editors.

CARLES TORNER

PHOTO: AUTHOR'S ARCHIVE

CARLES TORNER (born Barcelona, 1963) is a poet and writer. He has a PhD from the Paris VIII University and has chaired the Committee for Translation and Linguistic Rights of International PEN (1994-2004). He was director of the Literature and the Humanities Department at the Institut Ramon Llull (2004-2010) and is currently lecturer at the Faculty of Communication and International Relations Blanquerna (URL).

Torner has published several volumes of poetry: *In the White City* (1984, Amadeu Oller Award), *The Limits of Salt* (1984, Carles Riba Award), *The Angel of Plunder* (1990), *Life Afterwards* (1998, National Critics Award) and *Europe's Bride* (2008). He has also published a novel, *The Foreign Woman* (1997), the essay *Shoah, a Pedagogy of Memory* (2001) and *Babel's Arch* (2005), a book mixing narrative and essay, in the form of thirty-five letters to women from different countries who are struggling against the threats to their languages and cultures.

* * *

Pensem la mort al centre de la vida.
Cantem ben fort: cap fràgil cos colgat
sota la llei del sabre! On, l'honrat
bon ciutadà que accepta la mentida

al preu – al cost! – del dret al pit de dida
d'esquerpa llet? Els folls, alienat
germà, han dit camins de pau i blat.
Cap mot promès. Només sento la crida

al vent comú. Sabrem el goig d'un cos
en llibertat al pas marcat per ritmes
clars, col·lectius. La lluita: carn sens os

amunt, endins pel centre de la nit.
Obro el sarró: recullo instants sense istmes,
sense escorpins. Aprenc el foc al pit.

L'INFANT

Abans de tenir pressa, abans d'inventar l'hora,
abans dels dinosaures, de Tarzan, dels darwinistes,
abans dels metros, dels llaguts i dels trineus,
abans del mar, conqueridor sense cronistes,
i dels estels parant la taula dels desficis,
abans dels savis, les presons i els coliseus
i tota terra d'artificis,
quan tot era un mantell de buit molt fi
i el negre un sol color sense cap vora,
aquest dolor d'infant que plora
ja era aquí.

L'ÀNGEL DEL SAQUEIG

Com si la soledat dels homes i del temple
tingués mai un demà de festa i d'harmonia,
com si aquest ploviscó que creix fos un diluvi
que s'insinua amb por,

* * *

Let us think death into the centre of life.
And let's sing loud: no fragile body buried
under the law of the knife! Where is the honest,
decent citizen who accepts the lie

at the price – at the cost! – of his right, at the breast
of the wet-nurse, to rough milk? Fools, my estranged
brother, have spoken ways of peace and harvest.
Not a word have they promised. I hear only the moan

in the common wind. We will know the joy of a body
that is free, marching to the beat of clear,
collective rhythms. The fight: flesh with no bones

upon it, deep in the middle of the night.
I open the satchel: I gather instants with no land-bridge,
no scorpions. I learn the fire in the breast.

THE CHILD

Before being in a hurry, before they invented time,
before the dinosaurs, or Tarzan, before the Darwinists,
before the subways, before fishing boats, or sledges,
before the sea, conqueror without chroniclers,
and stars setting the table with anxieties,
before sages, prisons and coliseums,
and every land of artifice,
when everything was a fine cloak of emptiness
and black a single colour with no edge,
this pain that is a child weeping,
this was already here.

THE PLUNDERING ANGEL

As though the solitude of men and of the temple
were some day to bring days of celebration or harmony,
as though this growing drizzle were a flood
that creeps inside with fear,

com una veu que ens vol rebuig i escàndol,
arriba l'àngel del saqueig,
rabent, ales de foc que inflamen tot amb fúria,
revela l'ànima dels llibres,
fendeix l'espai ferit de grocs i blaus i flames,
crema el desig quan surt dels llavis del desig
i marxa amb so de perles en tempesta
mentre s'ensorra el temple.
Ens resta sols un viu dolor
damunt l'altar de la memòria.

POC ABANS DE L'INCENDI

I les cases cauran. Poc abans, als balcons,
les mestresses hauran desestès la bugada,
aquest cop cap enfora; llençols, bruses, pijames,
no seran recollits; deixaran que, lleus, planin,
voleiant pel carrer en un últim adéu,
fent-se un màgic tapís, clapejant les voreres.

En sec, cauran les cases. I el que hi hagi al darrere.
I el teatre sencer. Cremarem les disfresses
i entre el roig de les flames un cel brut i plorós
s'ajaurà pels carrers.
Els amics fugiran. Els amics i les llàgrimes
i tants ulls que han sabut desvetllar-me tants anys
quan la vida es llançava pels espadats del somni.
Restaré aquí tot sol,
amb els dits recremats de petons i paisatges,
amb no res tret del nom i del lliure estimar-te.

CIRC

Deixen la carpa enrere. Ella va absorta:
reveu dues acròbates que es troben
a gran alçada,
dos cossos drets, capiculats, verticalíssims,
lliscant amb peus de seda sobre el cable
damunt del buit.
        Ell va distret:

as a voice that wishes us to be reject and scandal,
the plundering angel comes: swift, with wings of fire setting
everything ablaze with fury,
reveals the soul of the books,
splits space wounded with yellows and blues and flames,
burns desire when it issues from the lips of desire
and marches with the sound of a storm of pearls
while the temple collapses.
All that is left to us is a piercing pain
on the altar of memory.

JUST BEFORE THE FIRE

And the houses will fall. Just before, on the balconies,
housewives will have taken down the washing,
outside, this time: sheets, blouses, pyjamas,
will not be brought back in; they will let them float, lightly,
flying over the street in a final farewell,
becoming a magic carpet, flecking the pavements.

Suddenly, the houses will fall. And whatever stands behind them.
And the entire theatre. The costumes will burn
and between the red of the flames a dirty, tearful sky
will lie down in the streets.
Friends will run away, the friends and the tears
and all those eyes who have for so many years kept me awake
when life was thrown away over cliffs of sleep.
I will stay here on my own,
my fingers burned by kisses and landscapes,
with nothing lost from the name, from the freedom to love you.

CIRCUS

They leave the Big Top behind. She is absorbed:
she sees again two acrobats who meet
at a great height,
two upright bodies facing each other, utterly straight,
sliding on silken feet along the cable
over the void.
           He is distracted:

no es treu dels ulls la trapezista alada,
el gest exacte dels turmells,
l'ample zim-zam de cabellera d'ombra
que escombrava la llum dintre el cercle del focus.

Han vist estels de foc:
saltaven com espurnes de les mans
d'un gran malabarista.
Han vist cavalls, camells i un elefant
ballant plegats sota el fuet del domador.
El pallasso era mut i ventríloc alhora:
parlava amb la veueta trista
del seu acordió.

«T'hi has fixat? El nen quasi plorava
quan ha sortit la ballarina a consolar el pallasso...»
«El nen, on és el nen?» Es giren,
el criden, s'atabalen, corren amunt i avall,
tornen a entrar a la carpa:
els músics, els pallassos, els camells
i tots els savis seuen en rotllana
i miren cap amunt, bocabadats.
Al cel del circ,
l'infant s'enfila al trampolí d'una paràbola
                                        i vola,
vola entre dos trapezis,
travessa ingràvid
el cercle encès del focus
damunt del buit.

OBJECTES

T'he treballat com un orfebre bíblic
que fila el fil de plata de l'amor
fins que, maldestre, el trenca.
T'he masegat com l'escultor makonde
que martelleja, exorcitzant-lo, l'eben,
fins a arrencar-ne el fosc, l'antic dimoni
que posseïa la matèria.
I t'he parlat com un poeta escèptic
que oblida amb paciència els versos revelats
per una llambregada entre dos cotxes,

he can't get out of his mind the winged trapeze-artist,
the precise movement of her ankles,
the ample to and fro of long hair full of shadow
sweeping the spotlight's luminous circle.

They have seen stars made of fire:
they leaped like sparks from the hands
of a great juggler.
They have seen horses, camels and an elephant
dancing together under the trainer's whip.
The clown was a dumb ventriloquist:
he spoke in the sad little voice
of his accordion.

"Did you notice? The child was almost crying
when the ballerina came out to comfort the clown..."
"The child? Where is he?" They turn around,
call him, grow anxious, rush hither and thither,
return to the Big Top, go in:
the musicians, clowns and camels
and all the wise men sit in a ring
and gaze upwards, mouths open.
At the the circus top
the child climbs on to the springboard of a parabola
and flies

flies between two trapezes,
weightlessly crossing
the fiery circle of the ring
above the void.

OBJECTS

I have worked you like a goldsmith in the Bible
who spins love's silver thread
until, cack-handed, he breaks it.
I have beaten you like the Makonde carver
who hammers at ebony, exorcising it
until he drags out the dark and ancient demon
the wood possessed.
And I've spoken to you like a sceptical poet
who patiently forgets the lines revealed
by a quick glance between two cars,

pels préssecs copejats sota la llum glaçada,
per un pessic de mort que es recargola
a sota una camisa,
i oblida en pau i amb perseverança
fins que s'imposen les paraules als seus llavis
i accepta el pòsit fràgil del sentit.

Avui t'he vist – imatge
que t'has girat a l'autobús –
com qui veu un objecte:
dos esperits de plata que es devoren
capiculats dins un joiell,
un estrafet dimoni agonitzant
que alliberava els cossos d'eben a la vida,
un vers escrit sota l'espasa del mutisme:
t'he treballat com un orfebre bíblic.

DIVISA

La llebre esquiva el tret del caçador
i ho crida als núvols foscos de l'afrau.
Ho escriu la pluja al fang de la tardor
i ho va llegint la fulla d'om quan cau.

La mare sola ho beu en el gorgol
d'ocultes fonts. Ho canta el fugitiu.
La sargantana ho prega al bat del sol.
Ho implora al cel, saltant, la truita al riu.

El mendicant ho diu parant la mà,
la traductora, quan escull rimar,
i l'escriptor, servint la llengua, eixit.

L'alzina ho clama al llamp que la fereix,
la lluna, al sol, i el grill ho repeteix:
contra la por, la veritat del crit.

by peaches lying bruised in an icy light,
by a pinch of death that huddles beneath a shirt,
and forgets in peace and with perseverance
until, when words impress themselves on his lips,
he accepts the fragile trace of feeling.

Today I saw you – image
of you turning round on the bus –
like one who sees an object:
two silver spirits devouring each other
head to tail inside a jewel,
a dying, deformed devil
setting life's ebony bodies free,
a line written under the sword of silence:
I have worked you like a goldsmith in the Bible.

DEVICE

The hare escapes the hunter with his gun
and shrieks it to the gorge's lowering cloud.
The rain traces it deep in autumn mud
and then the elm leaf reads it, drifting down.

The lonely mother drinks it from the gush
of hidden springs. The song of the man on the run.
The lizard's prayer in the pouring down of sun.
The trout, leaping, begs it of heaven and river's rush.

The beggar utters it with outstretched hands,
and the translator, choosing she will rhyme,
the writer, slave to language, rapt in dream.

The holm-oak shrieks it as the lightning wounds,
sun, moon, grasshopper say it, time after time:
in the face of fear, the only truth's a scream.

LA CAMIONETA VERMELLA

en record de Yael Langella

Vaig conduint. Quan sortim d'un revolt
veiem el nostre destí, entre pinars,
mirant cap a la vall: l'estesa
del cementiri de Collserola.
És un camí prou vell. En un sotrac
trontolla tot, el maleter repica,
que el duc ple de pilotes i canyes
de pescar, una manxa de bicicleta,
la cadireta de la nena… Fins i tot
quan ells no hi són, aquí ressonen els crits
dels meus fills que juguen o es barallen.
La camioneta va deixant sempre
un rastre de vida, desordenada,
acollidora, a l'espera d'un viatge
inesperat, com un piset ambulant
per carreteres i carrers.
Avui vaig ple de gom a gom:
al meu costat hi seu el vidu,
darrere els teus amics,
els més recents,
els més antics.

A la ciutat dels morts, haig d'esquivar
rams de roses de plàstic que el vent furiós
va arrossegant aquí i allà damunt l'asfalt.
Rambla dels morts amunt, voldria fer callar
el ressò de criatures, la vida exuberant
que duc sempre impregnada, que no s'adiu aquí.
Inútilment: s'escridassen, salten,
canten a plena veu. Entre torres de morts
arribem al teu lloc: un nínxol alt,
a tocar del cel. T'acomiadem
mirant amunt. La cinta que lliga el ram
de flors dels teus companys del PEN,
fuetejada al vent, la cinta rosa
adés es dreça com una llança, guiant
la vista cel amunt, adés es mou
com una mà oscil·lant
que ens diu adéu amics,
bon vespre amics,
adéu amics,
bon dia.

THE RED VAN

in memory of Yael Langella

I'm driving. When we come out of a bend
we see our destination, among pine woods,
looking towards the valley: the expanse
of the cemetery of Collserola.
It's quite an old road. Going over a bump
everything jolts about and the boot clangs,
because it's full of footballs and fishing-
rods, a bicycle handlebar,
our daughter's buggy… Even when
they're not present, my children's voices
ring out here, playing or quarrelling.
The red van always leaves in its wake
a trail of life, untidy,
welcoming, waiting for an unexpected
journey, like a tiny apartment
travelling along streets and highways.
Today it is full to overflowing:
beside me sits the widower,
behind are your friends,
the most recent,
and the oldest ones.

At the necropolis I have to dodge
wreaths of plastic roses which the furious wind
tosses hither and thither over the tarmac.
Travelling up the avenue of the dead, I would like to hush
the noise of children, the exuberant life
I carry and which saturates me, which is out of place here.
Hopeless: they shriek, jump about,
sing at the top of their voices. Among the towering dead
we arrive at your place: a lofty recess,
as high as the sky. We bid you farewell,
gazing upwards. The ribbon tying the bunch
of flowers from your colleagues at PEN,
whipped by the wind, the pink ribbon
now stands up straight like a lance, directing
the gaze upwards, now moves
like a hand waving
saying goodbye, my friends,
good evening, friends,
goodbye friends,
have a good day.

Quan, més tard, deixaré tothom a casa seva
ens quedarem tots sols, el cotxe i jo,
la meva camioneta vermella.
Hi sentiré de nou, eixordador, brogit
d'infants i al mig, nítidament, la teva veu.
En hebreu els parlaràs dels teus viatges,
en rus, en japonès, en alemany,
en àrab, en búlgar i italià i els meus fills picaran l'ham
i et desafiaran amb l'espetec de consonants
d'una paraula de zulú que van aprendre
l'estiu passat. Aturat al semàfor vermell
del carrer de Pentecosta, tornaré a sentir
la música de Kroke que ha sonat al funeral,
el llarg lament meditatiu
d'un violí. Llum verda. Engegaré,
l'acordió clavarà el seu esperó
en el contrabaix, es desbridarà
el violí i tots tres, amb mi, es revoltaran:
serà una dansa boja, enriolada, que tot s'ho endú
giravoltant. Els meus fills ja ballaran
taral·lejant la melodia, botant,
xisclant, i tu també riuràs,
ballant amb ells, Yael,
ballant amb el futur
per sempre més.
Amén.

GEST D'ABRAHAM

Fa uns quatre mil anys, algú va decidir
no matar més infants.

Potser va ser la mà de l'àngel, de l'intrús,
qui va aturar la mà aixecada amb el punyal
tot just abans del crim. Potser va ser la veu
interior.
            Potser.
                        Va ser en tot cas un gest:
deixar de matar infants.
O el contrari d'un gest: renúncia a aquell gest,
agemolida, íntima genuflexió
de la mirada.
Contra la mà de l'àngel damunt la seva mà,

Later, when I have taken everyone home,
we'll be on our own, the car and I,
my red van.
I'll hear again the deafening din
of children and, in their midst, your voice.
In Hebrew you'll tell them about your travels,
in Russian, in Japanese, in German,
in Arabic, Bulgarian and Italian and my children will swallow the bait
and challenge you with the clatter of consonants
of a Zulu word they learned
last summer. Stopped for a red light
on Pentecosta street, I'll hear again
the strains of Kroke's music that was played at the funeral,
the long, meditative lament
of a violin. Green light. I'll put the car in gear,
the accordion will dig its spurs into the double-bass, the violin
will kick up its heels and all three, plus me, will whirl about:
it will be a crazy dance, bursting with laughter, with everything
carried off spinning. My children will dance
humming the melody, skipping,
shrieking, and you too will be laughing,
dancing with them, Yael,
dancing with the future
for ever more.
Amen.

ABRAHAM'S GESTURE

About four thousand years ago someone decided
not to kill any more children.

Maybe it was the angel's hand, the intruder,
that stopped the raised hand with the knife
just before the crime. Maybe it was the voice
inside him.
       Maybe.
            In any case it was a gesture:
to leave off killing children.
Or the opposite of a gesture: the renouncing of that gesture,
humbled, intimate genuflexion
of the gaze.
Faced with the angel's hand above his own,

contra la veu que clama la genuflexió,
l'home va defallir.
                    Baixà el punyal.
                                        Salvà
l'infant.
            Abans, però, potser, amb el puny alçat,
mentre la veu de l'àngel l'eixordava, Abraham,
tancant els ulls, veié tot el futur alçat,
el temps com una onada abraonada:
lluita, pasqua, alliberament,
pelegrinatge, exili,
la presència elusiva de la veu que ara parla,
temples a un déu de pau,
promesa i profecia, combats de nit amb l'àngel,
anunciació, visitació, magníficat, infantament,
crucifixió i aparicions,
nens deportats, exterminats
a la diàspora europea,
màrtirs de cap a cap d'Amèrica Llatina,
guerres de religió a Jerusalem,
neteges ètniques a Bòsnia, crims a Txetxènia:
un riu d'infants cadàvers, un devessall
de torturats, morts, amputats,
guerres en nom d'aquell
que ara li atura el braç i que l'eixorda:
«Deixa de matar infants.»
                            Quina absurda promesa
pot fer-li aturar el gest?
                        «Deixa de matar infants!»
Quin crit interior l'assalta i l'esborrona?
I quin poder té el crit?
                        «Deixa de matar infants»,
ho repeteix el vent contra els cabells del noi
que se'l mira amb terror.
                        I l'home abaixa el braç.

DESTRADUIR EUROPA

És un dia clement, ple de llum amistosa.
Un diumenge d'estiu
he vist els taüts verds: dos-cents vuitanta-dos
d'aquells vuit mil.

faced with the voice demanding that he kneel,
the man gave way.
                          He lowered the knife.
                                              He spared
the child.
                    And yet before that, maybe, with knife poised,
while the angel's voice deafened him, Abraham,
closing his eyes, saw the future raised up,
time like a wave clasping him:
struggle, passover, a setting free,
pilgrimage, exile,
the elusive presence of the voice now speaking,
temples to a god of peace,
promise and prophecy, wrestling by night with the angel,
annunciation, visitation, magnificat, childbirth,
crucifixion and appearings,
children deported, exterminated
in the European diaspora,
martyrs the whole length of Latin America,
religious wars in Jerusalem,
ethnic cleansings in Bosnia, crimes in Chechnya:
a river of child corpses, an outpouring
of the tortured, dead, mutilated,
wars in the name of him
who now stops his arm and deafens him with:
"Cease killing children."
                          What absurd promise
can make him hold back his gesture?
                              "Cease killing children!"
What inner cry assaults him and makes his hair stand on end?
And what power does the cry possess?
                              "Cease killing children",
the wind echoes it in the boy's hair
as he stares up at him in terror.
                          And the man lowers his arm.

UNTRANSLATING EUROPE

"The day is mild, the light is generous."
One Sunday in summer
I saw the green coffins: two hundred and eighty-two
out of those eight thousand.

Part opaca de l'ombra,
imatge buida del que fou
Srebrenica, els ulls s'hi aferren, llisquen,
no veuen res.
Ja no veig res.
Agafo, amb els meus ulls, la pala.
Torno a les fosques.
I torno a tu pel crit que m'ho demana,
com si el camí i el crit
fossin un raig de llum recargolant-se en cerca
d'un alfabet futur. Com si el crit fossis tu,
veu, caminant-te:
ni un crit, i tot és crit.

Torno a les fosques, Bashkim,
perquè m'has demanat que explori
quina geografia oculta
recorre els versos que ara escric.
Aixeco doncs la pala,
em poso el casc d'espeleòleg,
encenc la lot dels salms
i al primer revolt dessota terra
t'hi trobo a tu, que llegeixes:
un esvoranc al mapa, només l'omplen
el titubeig i la compassió
intuïda als teus ulls. Què hi ha,
enllà? Faig quatre passos més avall,
al fons d'aquesta poesia
de la pressa: mapar com un cartògraf,
gosar poder enllestir el poema
que et demana un amic per a bastir un diàleg
amb escriptors d'arreu i trobar-te cara a cara
les mares que s'abracen
als taüts verds entorn dels quals
de Vukovar a Srebrenica
totes les veus són mudes
tota la veu
crema en poema
la filiació
pendent.

Què vol dir què vull dir què vols dir
quan travessem quan travesseu quan travessen la plaça
del mercat i Cracòvia

Solid part of the shadow,
empty image of what was once
Srebrenica, eyes that catch at it slide off,
see nothing.
Now I see nothing.
I reach, with my eyes, for the spade,
I go back to darkness.
And I go back to you for the cry demanded of me,
as though the road and the cry
were a ray of light curling in search
of some future alphabet. As though the cry were you,
voice, walking along:
not a single cry, and everything is a cry.

I go back to the darkness, Bashkim,
because you have asked me to explore
what secret geography
runs through the lines I now write.
So I shoulder my spade,
put on my miner's helmet,
switch on the light-beam of the psalms,
and at the first bump, underground,
it's you I find, reading:
a hole in the map, and the only thing to fill it
is the guessed-at hesitation and compassion
of your eyes. What is that,
down there? I go down four more paces,
to the depths of that poetry
of haste: mapping it like a cartographer,
delighting in being able to finish off the poem
a friend had asked you for to build a dialogue
with writers everywhere and find yourself face to face
with mothers embracing
the green coffins around which
from Vukovar to Srebrenica
all voices are dumb
the entire voice
burns in a poem
the question of sonship
pending.

What does it mean what do I mean what do you mean
when we cross when you cross when they cross
the market place and Krakov

sorgeix nua en obrir de bat a bat
la finestra, la pàgina:
era un dia clement, ple de llum amistosa.
A la terrassa del cafè, un alemany,
damunt dels seus genolls, tenia un llibre.
Vaig arribar a llegir-ne el títol:
«Mística per a debutants».

Però llegeixes Zagajewski
sense saber un borrall de polonès
tradueixes traduccions
com qui ribota amb la mirada els angles
de cases on viu gent, on criden als seus fills
que s'aixequin del llit
que no s'aixequin mai de taula abans d'haver acabat
que els llibres són sagrats
que se'ls mengin s'hi banyin s'hi acotxin s'hi aixopluguin
mentre els infants reclamen ulls com pidolaires
– uns ulls! –
perquè els consolin,
vas esmussant les cases
a cops de traduir uns versos traduïts
mentre l'origen se t'allunya
i em dius que tant se val, catalans, tant se val:
traduïm a la llengua d'un país sense forma
on ens esborren cada dia els vells contorns
encongits foradats estrafets sense fre
com podem traduir-los diluir-nos sobreviure?

demano uns altres ulls amb mans de pidolaire
– uns ulls per veure-hi!

Sense forma, ho entens?
De matí quan t'aixeques
no saps si encara avui tindràs
peus per calçar-te i al mirall la llengua
quequejant pastosa incerta tanmateix
sorgida del país
que és i no és
tanmateix tanmateix tanmateix
una veu sense veu va entonant lletanies
repeteix traduïdes paraules:

vaig arribar a llegir-ne el títol:
«Mística per a debutants».

rises up naked, as window, page,
are opened wide:
the day was mild, the light was generous.
The German on the cafe terrace
held a small book on his lap.
I caught sight of the title:
"Mysticism for beginners".

But you are reading Zagajewski
without knowing a word of Polish
you translate translations
like one who planes with his gaze the angles
of houses where people live, where they call to their children
to get out of bed
not to leave the table until they have finished
that books are holy
to be eaten to be bathed in to be tucked up in to be sheltered by
while children clamour for eyes like beggars –
for eyes! –
to console themselves,
you are busy blunting the sharp edges of houses
by translating lines of translated poetry
while the source recedes ever farther
and you tell me it doesn't matter, catalans, it doesn't matter:
we translate into the language of a country with no shape
where our old outlines are every day erased
shrunk, pierced, ceaselessly deformed
how may we translate them dilute ourselves survive?
I clamour for fresh eyes with beggar's hands –
eyes to let me see!

With no shape, do you understand it?
In the morning when you get up
you don't yet know whether today you'll have
feet to put shoes on and in the mirror your tongue
stuttering slurred uncertain and nevertheless
risen from the country
that is and is not
nevertheless nevertheless nevertheless
a voice without voice is chanting litanies
repeating translated words:

I caught sight of the title:
"Mysticism for beginners"

Vaig comprendre tot d'una que aquelles orenetes
que amb xiscles estridents anaven patrullant
pels carrerons de Montepulciano,
i el xiuxiueig de les converses d'intimidats turistes
de l'Europa de l'Est, que ara en diuen Central,
i tants bernats pescaires palplantats – ahir, abans d'ahir –
als arrossars, com monges petitones,
i el sistemàtic, lent crepuscle
esborrant els contorns de cases medievals
i els turons d'oliveres
abandonats al vent i la calitja,
i el cap d'una «Princesa desconeguda»
que havia vist al Louvre, i admirat

i el cap també de la meva princesa
la conec, jo la crid
i ella no es vol girar
i ella em crida al seu torn
mentre es regira al llit
ara faràs mapa'm,
                    Sara farà
riure els tres àngels
ara diràs té, cec, ets àrid,
                         ara
ve Rut s'ha tret la samarreta
i du un piercing al pit
amb una falç daurada
que en penja i dringa
i la desconeguda
m'ha citat amb tres rostres
i el tercer té per nom la temuda impaciència
l'amor és un saquet de lletres
passa la nit entre els teus pits
i es buida tot t'honora i és
infinita o no res la paciència

traduir Zagajewski el poema
desitjant esperant implorant que el poema
sigui allò que pot ser traduït
no la resta el que clama fora del teu abast
i fa néixer estrangers escopits a la platja
sense papers sota la llum daurada
sense paper ni tinta ni alfabet
només el plor que aprèn a ser una veu
el plor que infantarà l'absent

Suddenly I understood that the swallows
patrolling the streets of Montepulciano
with their shrill whistles
and the hushed talk of the timid travellers
from Eastern, so-called Central Europe
and the white herons standing – yesterday? the day before? –
like nuns in fields of rice,
and the dusk, slow and systematic
erasing the outlines of mediaeval houses
and olive trees on little hills,
abandoned to the wind and heat,
and the head of the Unknown Princess
that I saw and admired in the Louvre

and the head as well of my own princess
I know her, I call to her
and she does not want to turn round
and she calls to me in her turn
while she turns over in bed
you'll do it now take my picture.
                              Sarah will make
the three angels laugh
now you'll say here you are, blind man, you're dry,
                                                  now

Ruth comes has taken off her undergarment
and has one breast pierced
with a ring in the shape of a gold sickle
which dangles and chimes
and the unknown woman
has come to our *rendez-vous* with three faces
and the third one is called fearful impatience
love is a small bundle of letters
spends the night between your breasts
empties out everything, does you honour and
patience is infinite or nothing

translating Zagajewski the poem
wanting hoping imploring that the poem
may turn out to be what can be translated
not the remainder that which clamours beyond your reach
and causes foreigners to be born spewed up on the beach
without papers under the golden light
without paper or ink or alphabet
only the weeping that learns to be a voice
the weeping the absent one gives birth to

que fa néixer una mare
bellesa vida meva benvinguda
benvinguda bellesa
nadó que ja tens forma
de cop i volta
i tens nom
nom de dona,
Desconeguda, Sara, Rut,
ets la veu d'un llinatge
n'ha nascut una mare
sense papers amb nom la forma
esmunyedissa ploradora espeternega
rebel incrèdula claror
arrel llinatge absent
on creixem ens arbrem entronquem ens malpoden
a les branques s'ajoquen
consonants i vocals
pregàries cançons de bressol l'art
només l'art trenca el cercle
i el xiuxiueig de les converses d'intimidats turistes
de l'Europa de l'Est, que ara en diuen Central,
i tants bernats pescaires palplantats – ahir, abans d'ahir –
als arrossars, com monges,
i el sistemàtic, lent crepuscle
esborrant els contorns de cases medievals
i els turons d'oliveres
abandonats al vent i la calitja,
i el cap d'una «Princesa desconeguda»
que havia vist i admirat al Louvre,
i els vitralls d'esglésies com ales de papallones
clapejades de pol·len,
i el petit rossinyol que assajava la seva recitació
a frec de l'autopista,
i els viatges, qualsevol viatge,
qualsevol viatge vol dir també els viatges
que no has fet, que mai més no faràs
només l'art trenca el cercle
que vol recloure la destrucció dels musulmans
al crim de Srebrenica
fent-te triar el silenci pietós o bé l'obscena
banalització quan tots naixem
estrangers escopits a la platja sense papers

sense res per escriure el teu nom
Europa és el govern holandès dimitint

which causes a mother to be born
beauty my blessed life
blessed beauty
newborn child you already have a shape
all at once
and you have a name
a woman's name,
Unknown woman, Sarah, Ruth,
you are the voice of a lineage
from which a mother has been born
with no papers with the name
the slippery weeping kicking shape
rebellious incredulous clarity
root absent lineage
in which we grow afforest graft ourselves are badly pruned
in whose branches
vowels and consonants roost
with prayers cradle-songs art
art alone breaks the circle
and the hushed talk of the timid travellers
from Eastern, so-called Central Europe
and the white herons standing – yesterday? the day before? –
like nuns in fields of rice,
and the dusk, slow and systematic,
erasing the outlines of mediaeval houses
and olive trees on little hills
abandoned to the wind and heat,
and the head of the Unknown Princess
that I saw and admired in the Louvre,
and stained-glass windows like butterfly wings
sprinkled with pollen,
and the little nightingale practising
its speech beside the highway,
and any journey, any kind of trip,
any journey meaning also the journeys
you've never been on, never will go on
only art breaks the circle
that wishes to shut out the murdering of moslems
in the crime of Srebrenica
making you choose the pious silence or else obscene
banalisation in which we are all born
as foreigners spewed up on a beach with no papers

with nothing to write your name
Europe is the Dutch government resigning

és el gran Mazoviecki dimitint
són milers d'escriptors jugant a ser neutrals
mentre Dobrica Cosic escriu els fonaments
de la neteja ètnica,
és la dimissió l'anar esborrant el propi nom

i caure de genolls a la platja
d'aquest poema, Bashkim,
que no pot dir sencer el fracàs
en traduir a temps una paraula, fracassar
en saber quan és l'hora

en l'hora necessària quan cal cavar amb els ulls
i parir la pròpia mare
arrabassada

En una llibreria de Cracòvia
vaig llegir un títol: «Mística per a principiants»
Vaig comprendre tot d'una que la imatge
dels taüts verds amb mares abraçades, al diari,
i la invitació d'en Bashkim
que duu la geografia tatuada als seus ulls
i el meu país que no té forma
i el poema de Zagajewski
que no puc traduir
i el present permanent de Srebrenica
i aquell congrés del PEN prop del final del segle
que va ser l'escenari on poder dir el fracàs
per no perdre l'alè, la paraula,
i la petita falç damunt del camp d'estrelles
i el riure de tres àngels
i el vell saquet de lletres
que duus de nits entre els teus pits
i desnéixer, destraduir
Europa fins a l'origen
per tornar a sorgir amb elles,
per donar a llum la pròpia mare
i jo la crid
i ella no es vol girar
i els viatges, qualsevol viatge,
no eren res més que mística per a debutants,
el curs elemental, preludi
de l'examen que ha estat
ajornat.

it is the great Mazoviecki resigning
it is thousands of writers playing at being neutral
while Dobrica Cosic writes the foundations
of ethnic cleansing,
it is resignation this process of erasing people's names

and falling to one's knees on the beach
of this poem, Bashkim,
which cannot utter in its entirety the failure
to translate in time a single word, failing
to know when it is time

at the right time when you have to dig with your eyes
and give birth to your mother
uprooted

In a bookshop in Krakov
I read a title: "Mysticism for beginners"
I understood all at once that the image
of the green coffins embraced by mothers, in the newspaper,
and the invitation from Bashkim
who carries that geography tattooed in his eyes
and my country that has no shape
and the poem by Zagajewski
that I cannot translate
and the permanent present of Srebrenica
and that PEN conference at the end of the century
that was the setting in which to be able to speak of the failure
so as not to lose breath, speech,
and the little sickle over the field of stars
and the laughter of three angels
and the old bundle of letters
that you hold at night between your breasts
and to be unborn, to untranslate
Europe back to the source
so as to be able to rise up with them
to give birth to one's own mother
and I call her
and she doesn't want to turn round
and any journeys, any kind of trip,
are only mysticism for beginners,
the elementary course, prelude
to a test that's been
postponed.

Note: The lines in italics are an English translation by Clare Cavanagh from the
original Polish of the poem 'Mysticism for Beginners' by Adam Zagajewski.

GEMMA GORGA

PHOTO: AUTHOR'S ARCHIVE

GEMMA GORGA I LÓPEZ (born Barcelona, 1968) has a PhD in Philology from the University of Barcelona, where she works as a teacher. Her work is focused primarily in the field of Medieval and Renaissance literature. She has published four collections of poetry: *Ocellania* (Barcelona, 1997), *El desordre de les mans* (The Hands' Disorder, Lleida, 2003), *Instruments òptics* (Optical Instruments, València, 2005) and *Llibre dels minuts* (Book of Minutes, Barcelona, 2006). The latter appeared in Catalan-Spanish bilingual edition (*Libro de los minutos y otros poemas*, Valencia, 2009, translated by V. Berenguer). She has also written, in collaboration with Antonio Lozano, an essay entitled '*La cuina natural*' (The Natural Kitchen, Barcelona, 2004). She has participated in various festivals and poetry readings in the Basque Country, Slovenia, Germany, Poland, Finland, Venezuela and Chile. Following a three month residence with the Sanskriti Foundation in New Delhi, she is currently working on a translation of contemporary anglophone Indian poets.

RETORN

Jo era petita i m'havien de dir què fer,
cap on anar, com somriure davant d'una xocolatina,
com agafar la forquilla, com agafar la vida,
com no xarrupar la sopa de galets,
què llegir als estius i com balancejar la cua de cavall.

Tant era el meu desig d'un vestit color neula
tot esponjat de farbalans i mànigues càlides.
Jo era petita
i això significava que plovia
i això significava que els rellotges estaven enfangats
i això significava que aquell dia s'esqueia el vestit verd
i raspós com la mirada de la Cruela de Vil.

Jo era petita com una formiga.
Com una formiga, sí,
tan menuda que sovint em perdia
entre els plecs de la faldilla de la meva mare.
Un cop em van trobar sota la sivella
de la seva sandàlia de platja,
vivint entre la sorra i la pell.

I ara em dic:
tu eres petita,
eres tan petita,
tu eres petita
com haguessis pogut ser
        una agulla d'estendre,
        un pinyó estès a terra
        o una finestra plena de neu,
si no fos perquè els altres sempre m'ho recorden
i així em defineixen encara avui:
tu eres petita.

HORÒSCOP

L'alfàbrega agonitza en un test esquerdat de terrissa.
A cops de pluja, el rostre clar de les finestres s'encega.
Agost, i les orenetes ja enfilen camí.
La veu escanyada del telèfon ha emmudit

GOING BACK

I was small and they had to tell me what to do,
where to go, how to smile when offered a chocolate,
how to take hold of my fork, how to take hold of life,
how not to slurp noodle soup,
what to read in the summertime and how to swing my pony-tail.

I had a great longing for a dress the colour of wafer-biscuits,
puffed up with flounces and warm sleeves.
I was small
and that meant that it rained
and that meant that the clocks were wrong
and that meant that that day there appeared the dress
that was as green and scratchy as one glance from Cruella De Vil.

I was as small as an ant.
Yes, as an ant,
so tiny that I was often lost
among the pleats of my mother's skirt.
Once they found me under the buckle
of the sandals she wore on the beach,
living between sand and skin.

And now I tell myself:
you are small,
you are so small,
you are small
so that you might have been
a clothes-peg,
a pine-nut lying on the ground
or a window covered in snow,
if it weren't for the others who always remind me of it
and still define me thus today:
you are small.

HOROSCOPE

The basil is dying in a cracked earthenware pot.
With the beating rain, the windows' clear face turns blind.
August, and the swallows are already on their way.
The telephone's hoarse voice has grown dumb

i ni tan sols els llibres s'avenen a concedir-me
el càlid consol de la paraula.
La nit m'embruta els llençols estesos
i les veïnes em tafanegen la correspondència.
L'alegria ha fugit sense avís
– ni una breu nota enganxada al mirall –
i els plats s'escantonen quan hi aboco el sopar.
L'home que estimo ja no dorm al meu llit
ni mossega la poma que jo li enceto.
Ja no recordo cap pel·lícula antiga
capaç d'alliberar-me fins al plor.

Aquest cop
els auguris celestes
parlen ben clar:
no sé quina posició ocupa la lluna,
però ha arribat,
sense més dilacions,
l'hora definitiva de partir.

PARLA L'ANCIANA PENÈLOPE

Ulisses, absent

Una altra tardor a ciutat
amb els dies que s'escurcen!

Darrere el finestró
guaito les orenetes
com marxen,
l'estesa de terrats
que es cavalquen sense fi,
les teulades humides
on habita l'ombra
sinuosa dels gats.

Lluny, una mà
escapça lilàs
i en serva la llavor
per a l'estiu.

La veïna, natura diligent,
estén llençols tibants
al vent autumnal.

and not even books agree on allowing me
language's warm consolation.
Night dirties the sheets I hung out
and my neighbours pry into my mail.
Happiness has fled without warning –
not even a brief note pinned to the mirror –
and the dishes get chipped when I serve the dinner.
The man I love no longer sleeps in my bed
or eats the apple I broach for him.
I can't think of any old film
capable of setting me free to weep.

This time
the heavenly portents
speak all too clearly:
I don't know what quarter the moon is in,
but there has come,
with no more shilly-shallying,
the right moment for departure.

THE AGED PENELOPE SPEAKS

   Ulysses, absent

Another autumn in the city
and the days dwindling!

Behind the shutter
I watch the swallows,
their departures,
the spread of fields
galloping away endlessly,
the damp roofs
inhabited by cats
with their sinuous shadow.

Far off, a hand
is cutting back the lilac
and keeping the seed
for summer.

The woman next-door, diligent soul,
hangs out taut sheets
in the autumn wind.

En aquestes hores encalmades
trec les agulles
i treno una bufanda
amb el cabdell
dels anys viscuts.

Perquè no me'n sé avenir, d'aquest fred,
d'aquest enuig de tot i per tot
que duc clavat com una estella.
D'aquesta buidor de tants anys viscuts
a l'ombra de l'home.
Jo, absent de mi.
A l'ombra del record.

Però acabarà la tardor
i jo també marxaré.
Desaré les agulles,
desfaré el que he trenat
i, mar enllà,
aprendré
a oblidar
Ítaca.

PEDRES

Si la veu pogués sortir a les fotografies
com hi surt l'ombra o la tendresa – tot i ser
realitats més vulnerables –, sentiria
un cop més el meu pare explicant-me que, abans
de collir una pedra, cal fer-la rodolar
amb el peu o amb una branca per espantar
els escorpins que s'hi amaguen com punxes seques.
Mai no vaig preocupar-me'n. Perquè tenir sis
anys era senzill, senzill com morir-se. En tots
dos casos, no hi havia més secret que l'aire:
respirar-lo o no respirar-lo, com si l'ànima
fos plena de diminuts alvèols que s'obren
i es tanquen. El primer escorpí que vaig veure
va ser al llibre de ciències naturals,
atrapat per sempre entre les pinces severes
del temps. De vegades, però, els llibres no expliquen
tota la veritat, com si no la sabessin

In these hushed hours
I get out my needles
and weave a shawl
with the skein
of the lived years.

Because I can't resign myself to it, this coldness,
this weariness of everything and in everything
that I carry nailed to me like a splinter.
This emptiness from so many years lived
in the man's shadow.
An I, absent from myself.
In memory's shadow.

But autumn will end
and I too will leave.
I will put away my needles,
I will unravel what I have woven
and, over the seas,
I will learn
to forget
Ithaca.

STONES

If the voice could come out of photographs
in the same way as shadow or tenderness – even though
these are more vulnerable realities – I would hear
again my father explaining to me how, before
you pick up a stone, you should roll it
with your foot or with a branch to frighten away
the scorpions that hide under it like dry thorns.
I never worried about them. Because being six
years-old was easy, as easy as dying. In both
matters, there was no secret other than the air:
to breathe it or not to breathe it, as though the soul
were full of diminutive alveoli that open
and close. The first scorpion I saw
was in a book on natural history,
caught forever between the severe pincers
of time. Sometimes, however, books don't explain
the whole truth, as though they don't know it

o l'haguessin oblidat camí de la impremta.
Aràcnid que té el cos dividit en abdomen
i cefalotòrax. Res no hi deia del sol
ardent a la llengua, de la por, de l'espiga
travessada al coll. Jo no sabia llavors
que les paraules són immensos icebergs
que oculten sota les aigües glaçades molt
més del que mostren. Com la paraula *escorpí*.
I ara, mentre el telèfon sona insistentment
– un crit agut de matinada –, mentre em llevo,
encenc el llum, acosto la mà al seu cos blanc
de plàstic que brilla com una pedra al sol,
mentre el despenjo, i dic sí?, i algú em diu que ets mort,
jo només penso en els escorpins, en allò
que volies dir-me quan repeties *fes*
rodar les pedres, sisplau, fes rodar les pedres.

JOYEUX NOËL

Aquesta habitació d'hotel ens conté com una capsa
de Nadal que ningú no tornarà a obrir. Es perdrà el record
de la poma a mig mossegar, el mapa que es neguiteja
damunt el llit, el bitllet d'avió que ens retornarà
on no volem retornar, el desig de tu encenent-se i apagant-se
com les llumetes del carrer. I, als peus de la finestra, les sabatilles
que ens observen, pacients i manses com un petit ramat d'ovelles.
Em pregunto si les habitacions d'hotel han après a celebrar
el Nadal. Per si de cas, aplego les serradures d'un dia gris
i les escampo entre els llençols, mentre tu aportes humitats
de molsa i retalles peixets de plata perquè llisquin sota els ponts
del meu cos. És estrany que aquesta ciutat sigui París,
dius. I mentre proves a orientar-te enmig del desordre
de les meves mans, la tarda es fon com un grapat de neu.

Aviat la nit ens caurà al damunt amb un cop sec
i ens trencarà l'ànima a miques: dues figuretes
de fang oblidades en una capsa de Nadal.

or had forgotten it on the way to the printers.
Arachnid having the body divided between abdomen
and cephalothorax. Nothing was said about the burning
sun of the tongue, of fear, of the spike
piercing the throat. I was unaware then
that words are huge icebergs
that conceal under icy waters much
more than they show. Like the word *scorpion.*
And now, while the telephone rings insistently –
a piercing early morning cry – while I get up,
turn on the light, stretch out my hand to its white
plastic body shining like a stone in the sun,
while I lift it, and say yes? and a voice tells me you are dead,
all I can think of are those scorpions, and what
you wanted to tell me when you repeated *make*
the stones roll away, please, make the stones roll away.

JOYEUX NOËL

This hotel room contains us like a Christmas
present which no one will come and open. The memory
of the half-eaten apple will be lost, the map lying anxiously
on the bed, the plane ticket which will take us back
to where we don't want to go, the desire for you coming on
and off like the lights in the street. And, below the window, the slippers
that watch us, patient and gentle as a small flock of sheep.
I wonder whether hotel bedrooms have learned to celebrate
Christmas. Just in case, I gather the sawdust of a grey day
and scatter it among the sheets, while you bring the dampness
of moss and cut out little silver fish so they can slip under
the bridges of my body. It is strange that this city should be Paris,
you say. And while you try to find your way among my
hands' disorder, the evening melts like a handful of snow.

Soon night will fall upon us with a sharp blow
and will smash our soul into atoms: two little figures
made of clay, forgotten inside a Christmas present.

DESCANS

La miro, menuda com és, entre els meus dits,
rodona i blanca com les llunes que pintava
a l'escola quan no sabia que el dolor pren
forma esfèrica i sempre torna a començar.
Ara és la llengua qui la mira, la interroga
en la foscor humida de la boca, la deixa
finalment passar, creuar boscos de saliva
que la duran al país de la por. Però
ella coneix els camins sense haver-hi estat
mai, ella, menuda com és, rodona i aspra,
sap en quina direcció queda la vena
que pateix, com adormir lentament el cor,
com empolsimar els capil·lars, com desteixir
els teixits. On ha après el pacient ofici
de la misericòrdia? Ella, menuda,
rodona i lenta com les llunes que pintava
a escola quan no sabia que el descans pren
forma esfèrica i sempre torna a començar.

ENS VAM OBLIDAR

Ens vam oblidar de donar corda
al rellotge de les nostres nits.
I ara mira els cossos, encallats
com rodes dentades que no saben
acoblar-se, provant de reprendre
el constant moviment giratori
que tenen la terra, l'huracà,
la dansa i la serp. La vida volta
sobre si mateixa al ritme cec
de l'esfera. I ara tu assenyales
les dotze de la nit, jo les dotze
del migdia, aturats ja per sempre
com dues agulles rovellades
que mai no tornaran a creuar-se
camí de l'amor, camí de l'odi.
Era senzill. I vam oblidar-ho.

REST

I look at her, small as she is, between my fingers,
round and white like the moons I used to paint
at school when I didn't know that pain adopts
a spherical shape and always goes back and begins again.
Now it is the tongue that looks at her, questions her
in the damp dark of the mouth, letting her go
at last, crossing woods made of saliva
which will bring her to the land of fear. But
she knows the way without ever having been there
in her life, she, small as she is, round and harsh,
she knows which way lies the vein
that aches, how to send the heart slowly to sleep,
how to sprinkle dust on capillaries, how to unravel
what has been woven. Where has she learned
mercy's patient craft? She, so small,
round and slow as the moons I used to paint
at school when I didn't know that rest adopts
a spherical shape and always goes back and begins again.

WE FORGOT

We forgot to wind up
the clock of our nights.
And now look at our bodies jammed
like cog-wheels that do not know
how to engage, trying to take up
the constant gyratory movement
shared by the earth, the hurricane,
the dance and the snake. Life turns
upon itself like the blind rhythm
of the sphere. And now you are striking
twelve o'clock midnight, and I, twelve
noon, now stopped for ever
like two rusty hands
that will never again cross each other's
love path, hate path.
It was a simple matter. And we forgot it.

FÒSFOR

Obro la capsa i els vaig extraient, un rere
l'altre, sense aturar-me. Encendre'ls és senzill:
s'agafen primer amb delicadesa entre els dits
i es freguen un instant contra una superfície
rugosa —com ara les parets de la nit,
els relleus de la memòria. De vegades
em pregunto d'on em ve aquest amor pels gestos
inútils, si deu ser malaltia o potser
benedicció: veure que res no serveix
de res, i seguir insistint, malgrat tot, seguir
cremant la fusteta prima dels mots que extrec
de la capsa amb delicadesa, un rere l'altre,
sense aturar-me. Apagar-los és tan senzill
com encendre'ls: únicament cal comptar fins
a tres, i despertar. De la gran lluminària
només en resta un grapat de petits cadàvers
calcinats que ara s'escampen sobre la pàgina
en blanc, i un estrany gust de fòsfor a l'arrel
de l'ànima, al centre exacte on neix el llenguatge.

PETIT CONTE

L'abella se m'acostà als llavis per dictar-me
l'inici d'un poema trobat a l'atzar
entre les síl·labes dolces del taronger.
Hauria estat senzill tancar els ulls i assentir
si no fos perquè ningú no em va ensenyar mai
a acceptar un miracle. Sé perfectament
com s'han de posar les mans per rebre una poma
enverinada, sé com s'ha d'inclinar el coll
per sentir la lenta mossegada vermella
de la nit, com s'acumula la crueltat
al fons de tots els miralls. Quines són les mans,
però, amb què es pren una ofrena? Com cal obrir-les
per acceptar el do inesperat? L'endemà
sempre és massa tard: l'abella no hi és, no queden
flors en cap taronger, i les síl·labes no troben
l'ordre adequat per indicar el final feliç.

PHOSPHORUS

I open the box and start taking them out, one after
another, without stopping. Lighting them is easy:
you hold them delicately between your fingers
and strike them for an instant against a rough
surface – against the walls of night,
the raised reliefs of memory. Sometimes
I wonder where this love for pointless gestures
stems from, if it must be an illness or perhaps
a blessing: to see that it's of no earthly use,
yet going on insisting, in spite of everything, on
burning the slender matchstick of words that I take
delicately out of the box, one after another,
without stopping. Extinguishing them is as easy
as lighting them: you need only count up to
three, and then wake up. Out of the great illuminations
all that's left is a handful of tiny, charred
corpses that now spread over the blankness
of the page, and a strange whiff of phosphorus at the root
of the soul, at the exact centre where language is born.

LITTLE STORY

The bee came close to my lips to dictate to me
the beginning of a poem found by chance
among the sweet syllables of the orange tree.
It would have been simple to shut my eyes and agree
if it weren't that nobody ever showed me
how to accept a miracle. I know perfectly well
how to place my hands to receive a poisoned
apple, I know how to bend my neck
to feel the slow crimson bite
night makes, how cruelty accumulates
in the depths of every mirror. With what hands,
however, should a gift be taken? How to open the hands
to accept the unexpected gift? The following day
it is always too late: the bee has vanished, no flowers
remain on any orange tree, and the syllables can't find
the proper order to show what the happy ending might be.

ATERRATGE

Contemplat des d'una certa distància,
diries que el món és un lloc amable
on habitar, una petita maqueta
de joguina on cada element encaixa
sense dolor – perquè les cicatrius
només s'aprecien de molt a prop,
quan enfoques amb la lent microscòpica
de les preguntes incautes i veus
tot allò que no creies que existís.
Des de l'avió, en canvi, la ciutat
sembla feta amb tendresa, com si algú
hagués anat col·locant els terrats
de pissarra, retallant els parterres,
decidint la direcció del fum,
construint les figures geomètriques
que brillen al sol. Algun artesà
minuciós ha introduït les peces
amb llargues pinces de rellotgeria
dins aquesta immensa ampolla de vidre.
El privilegi de ser observador,
però, dura poc. Quina és la distància
prudent per viure sense prendre mal,
sense trencar o ser trencat? Tard o d'hora,
l'avió inicia el descens al centre
candent de la matèria, travessa
la membrana de la seguretat
i aterra enmig del tràfec de la sang,
enmig de tu mateix, de mi, de tots
nosaltres, suficientment a prop
per fer-nos mal, estrets i neguitosos
com petits bacteris, buscant el rètol
d'un verd lluminós que ens ha d'indicar
sortida immediata cap a enlloc.

PARC D'ATRACCIONS

Sé prou bé on he d'anar aquesta tarda si vull
trobar-me amb la tristesa. És sorprenent la seva
disponibilitat – l'agenda plena d'hores
lliures – quan es tracta de mi. Quedem en veure'ns

LANDING

Seen from a certain distance
the world, you'd say, is a pleasant place
to live, a small maquette
for a toy in which each element fits
painlessly – because the scars
can be seen only when close up,
when you focus with the microscopic lens
of reckless questions and you see
everything you never believed existed.
From the plane, on the other hand, the city
seems made with tenderness, as though someone
had gone about putting in place the roofs
with their slates, outlining the flower-beds,
deciding which way the smoke should blow,
building the geometric shapes
that shine in the sun. Some painstaking
craftsman has introduced the pieces
with long, clockmaker's pliers
into this vast glass bottle.
The privilege of being an observer,
however, does not last long. What is the sensible
distance for living without taking hurt,
without breaking or being broken? Early or late,
the plane begins its descent to the white-hot
heart of matter, passes through
the safety membrane
and lands amid the hustle and bustle of blood,
in the midst of you yourself, of me,
of all of us, sufficiently close
to do us harm, cramped and anxious as we are
like tiny bacteria, searching for the sign
lit up in green which should tell us
the immediate exit to nowhere.

AMUSEMENT PARK

I know only too well where I have to go this evening if I want
to meet up with sadness. Its availability is surprising –
its diary full of empty spaces – when I am
the one concerned. We agree to meet

a dalt de tot. S'enlaira la sínia, lenta
i silenciosa com un immens rellotge
còsmic que el vent accionés de tant en tant.
Lluny, submergida en les aigües de la nit, brilla
la ciutat amb les seves escates daurades,
milers de boques mudes que s'obren i es tanquen
mentre neden pels corrents glaçats de la vida.
Quant temps fa que giravolto en aquesta sínia,
ara tan a prop del món, ara tan distant?
Com un astronauta perdut en l'espai, busco
un cable que em lligui a la respiració
dels altres, oxigen calent per als pulmons
que pregunten. Em miro la mà dreta, em miro
la mà esquerra, i trigo anys a cobrir la distància.

EL CEL SOBRE BERLÍN

No em preguntis el com ni el perquè. De vegades
hi ha coloms que equivoquen el camí, travessen
una finestra, una cortina, un mirall mig
obert, i res no pot evitar que s'escampin
pels cels transparents de l'ànima, com s'escampen
els colors de l'aquarel·la sota la gota
fortuïta d'aigua. No em preguntis el com
ni el perquè d'aquests errors, ni tan sols si són
errors. Com podríem saber de qui és la mà
que obre els miralls, de qui la mà que precipita
l'aigua? De vegades, la vida s'equivoca
de peça, mou blanca per negra, i aleshores
apareix una àliga sota l'abric, una
paraula en llavis d'una abella, un àngel trist
assegut en una bugaderia. Diuen
que és una cosa que ens passa a tots, no només
als qui tenen ales. Reconforta saber-ho.
Reconforta saber que l'error forma part
de nosaltres, que ens sosté com l'aire o la sang,
que els millors encontres són en realitat
pèrdues o confusions, atzars que passen
a mil metres d'altitud sobre les ciutats
oblidades, allà on les paraules s'eleven
com glòbuls efervescents, i desapareixen.

above everything. The wheel rises, slow
and silent like a huge cosmic clock
that the wind operates from time to time.
Far-off, submerged in the waters of night, the city
shines with its golden scales,
thousands of dumb mouths opening and closing
while they swim through life's icy currents.
How long have I been going round on this wheel,
now so close to the world, now so far away?
Like an astronaut lost in space, I search for a cable
that may connect me to the breathing
of others, warm oxygen for the beseeching lungs.
I look at my right hand, I look
at my left hand, and it takes me years to cover the distance.

THE SKY ABOVE BERLIN

Don't ask me about the whys or wherefores. Sometimes
there are pigeons that lose their way, pass through
a window, a curtain, a half-open
mirror, and nothing can prevent them spreading
through the soul's transparent skies, just as water-
colour tints spread through a drop of water fallen
by chance. Don't ask me about the whys
or wherefores of these mistakes, or even if they are
mistakes. How can we know whose hand it is
that opens mirrors, or whose hand spills
the water? Sometimes, life moves the wrong
piece, moves white instead of black, and then
there appears an eagle beneath the coat, a
word on the lips of a bee, a sad angel
sitting in a laundry. It is said
that this is something that happens to everyone, not just
to those who have wings. It's comforting to know that.
It's comforting to know that the mistake is a part
of us, that it sustains us like air or blood,
that the best encounters are actually
losses or muddles, chances that happen
three thousand feet up above forgotten
cities, there where words rise
like effervescent bubbles, and vanish.

LLARG RECORREGUT

Per les vies van els trens i els poemes.
Van de dia i van de nit. Finestretes
perquè respiri la llum – cada tres
segons, tres segons. La velocitat
es cargola a les oïdes com una
llarga cua de sirena. Empassar-se
una paraula per tornar a sentir-hi.
A les andanes algú mou la mà,
algú, qui. Trens plens de mercaderies,
trens de passatgers, trens de bestiar,
trens de lliteres, trens de deportats.
Inesperadament, el túnel tanca
els ulls. Trontollen les ombres, feixugues
com maletes massa plenes d'arrels.
I descarrila aquest poema absurd
que parlava – em sembla – de la distància.

TRAJECTE

Sóc un peix tancat en una bosseta
de plàstic, amb l'aigua i l'oxigen justos
per recórrer eficaçment el trajecte
que algú ha determinat (no sé ben bé
d'on, no sé tampoc cap a on). Hi ha qui
diu que venim de càlids oceans
plens de mareperles, coralls calcaris
on s'amaga la memòria, tendra
encara com un crustaci acabat
de néixer. També hi ha qui diu que ens porten
a immenses peixeres de color blau
cel, a la joia de la ingravidesa,
a la mà que ens alimenta i acull.
Vés a saber què hi haurà de cert més
enllà d'aquest trajecte, més enllà
dels límits específics d'una bossa
de plàstic transparent contra la qual
aixafo el nas. Quan miro enfora, l'única
escalfor que percebo és la del meu
propi alè, aquest ritme respiratori
que constitueix la sola certesa.

LONG JOURNEY

Along the tracks run the trains and the poems.
They run by day and they run by night. Little windows
so the light can breathe – every three
seconds, three seconds. The speed
curls into your ears like the long tail
of a mermaid. Swallowing
a word so as to hear it there once more.
On the platforms someone waves,
someone, who. Goods trains stuffed to the gunwales,
passenger trains, trains pulling cattle-trucks,
trains full of stretchers, trains of deportees.
Without warning, the tunnel closes
its eyes. Shadows stagger, heavy
as suitcases too full of roots.
And this absurd poem derails,
speaking – I think – about distance.

DISTANCE

I am a fish enclosed in a small plastic
bag, with just enough water and oxygen
to last the distance
that someone has planned (I don't quite know
from where, nor to what place). Someone says
that we come from warm oceans
full of mother-of-pearl, of calcareous corals
where memory hides, still
as tender as a newly emerged
crustacean. Someone also says that we are carried
to huge fish-ponds as blue as
the sky, to the joy of weightlessness,
to the hand that feeds and welcomes us.
Who knows what is certain
beyond this journey, beyond
the specific limits of a transparent
plastic bag against which
I press my nose. When I look outside, the only
heat I am aware of is that of my
own breath, this breathing rhythm
that constitutes the only certainty.

UNA DONA

Una dona planxa aprofitant l'última
llum que entra per la finestra. Convoca
les peces damunt la post, mulla els dits
molt lleument en aigua freda, les ruixa,
les marca amb el vapor triangular,
les pestanyes se li omplen de boira.
A fora, la ciutat també s'aplana
sota el crepuscle, com si els edificis
es desfessin en rius de metall fos.
De nit, a les fosques, segueix planxant,
planxa les flors, les rajoles de casa,
les parpelles que no saben tancar-se,
aquesta por nostra de cada dia.
A trenc d'alba, quan encara dormim,
ens treu l'ànima i l'allisa, del dret
i del revés, fins a esborrar-ne tot
plec insidiós, l'estigma del dubte.
I així, en llevar-nos el matí llueix
fresc com gespa acabada de tallar,
i les finestres no tenen lleganyes,
i l'esmorzar ens acull en el seu cercle
íntim i dolç com nata. Són les vuit.
Ens deixem transportar fins a la feina.
Amb la casa buida, ella entra i recull
dels peus del llit la muntanya de roba
bruta, el rebrec de les nostres ruïnes.
Rere el vapor dels segles, una dona
planxa aprofitant l'última claror.

MAGRANA

L'esgrano amb els dits i salten tot de records
sobre la llum gebrada del marbre. Petits,
encesos com bombetes vermelles de fira,
asprosos com la llengua felina del temps
que ens convida a seure a taula per engolir-nos
d'una bocada. La magrana torna cada
final de tardor, disposada a devastar-nos
una nit qualsevol, mentre som a la cuina
distrets amb el sopar: molt lleument va tacant-nos

A WOMAN

A woman is ironing, making the most
of the last of the light from the window. She gathers
the garments on the ironing-board, dips her fingers
lightly in cold water, sprinkles the clothes,
pressing them with the triangle of steam,
and her eyelashes fill with vapour.
Outside, the city too smooths itself out
in the dusk, as though the buildings
might be coming apart in rivers of molten metal.
In the night, in the darkness, she goes on ironing,
she irons the flowers, the tiles in the house,
the eyelids that don't know how to close,
this daily fear of ours.
At daybreak, while we're still asleep,
she pulls out our soul and smooths it, on the right
side and the wrong side, until she has erased from it
every insidious crease, the stigma of doubt.
And so, when we get up, the morning shines
as fresh as a lawn that has just been cut,
and the windows are free from smears,
and breakfast welcomes us into its circle
as intimate and sweet as cream. It's eight o'clock.
We let ourselves be carried to work.
With the house empty, she comes in and picks up
from the foot of the bed the pile of dirty clothes,
the crumpledness of our ruins.
Behind the steam of centuries, a woman
is ironing, making the most of the last of the light.

POMEGRANATE

My fingers pluck out the seeds and they spurt full of memories
on to the icy light of the marble counter. Tiny,
glowing like ruddy fairground lights,
rough as the cat's tongue of time
that invites us to come to the table to swallow us
in one mouthful. The pomegranate returns
every end of autumn, ready to ruin
any night of ours, while we are in the kitchen
busy with supper: very lightly it sets about staining

els dits amb aquell color pensatiu i tèrbol,
el color que tenen les hores que no acaben
de coagular, el color obert de la memòria.

LLIBRE DELS MINUTS (fragments)

4

¿Pots dibuixar un gat sense aixecar el llapis del paper – l'orella, la
corba tèbia del llom, la blanor del ventre, el nas, novament l'orella
– ? ¿Pots cartografiar les constel·lacions de l'hemisferi nord sense
aixecar el dit del cel, anar d'Andròmeda a Cassiopea, de Cassi-
opea a l'Óssa Major, i tornar a Andròmeda sense que es trenqui
el fil? Al capdavall, així és la vida, un passatemps, un passar el
temps que requereix la màxima habilitat per fer-la sencera d'un
sol traç. Per molt que la mà se t'entumeixi de fred i desemparan-
ça, recorda't de no aixecar el llapis.

7

QUAN era petita, li agradava tapar el vidre de la llanterna amb la
mà i mirar a contraclaror el perfil borrós dels dits, d'un vermell
aigualit, els ossets quiescents com crisàlides, la seda blanca de la
pell. Constantment aquell desig que la llum li travessés la carn i
li arribés ben endins del cor, com si tota ella fos un fanalet xinès
de paper fi. Amb els anys va entendre, però, que al centre de la
rosa sempre és de nit.

13

PESAVEN el cos uns minuts abans de morir. Pesaven el mateix cos
uns minuts després de morir. Una simple sostracció matemàtica
els havia d'indicar el pes de l'ànima. Hi penso, ara, mentre sos-
tinc el llibre nou entre les mans, les paraules encara untoses com
les plomes d'un ocell nascut de poc. I em pregunto si, un cop
llegit, també pesarà menys. Com un cos quan perd l'ànima.

our fingers with that pensive, dubious
colour the hours wear that never end up
clotting, the open colour of memory.

BOOK OF MINUTES (extracts)

4

CAN you draw a cat without lifting the pencil from the paper?
– the ear, the warm curve of the flank, the softness of the belly,
the nose, the ear again – ? Can you map the constellations of the
northern hemisphere without lifting your finger from the sky, go
from Andromeda to Cassiopeia, from Cassiopeia to the Great Bear,
and back to Andromeda without breaking the thread? In the end,
that's life, a pastime, a passing of time that requires the greatest
skill in order to do it in one stroke. However numb your hand may
grow with cold and weakness, remember not to lift the pencil.

7

WHEN she was small she liked to cover the glass on the lamp with her
hand and stare at the vague outline of her fingers, backlit, of a watery
red, the little bones lying still as chrysalids, the white silk of the skin.
She was always possessed by the desire that the light should pierce her
flesh and reach right inside her heart, as though the whole of her were
a chinese lantern made of fine paper. With the passing years, however,
she came to understand that at the heart of the rose it is always night.

13

THEY weighed the body a few minutes before death. They weighed
the same body a few minutes after death. A simple mathematical
subtraction was to tell them the weight of the soul. I think of that,
now, while I hold the new book in my hands, the words still sticky
like a newly-hatched fledgling. And I wonder whether, once it is
read, it will also weigh less. Like a body when it loses the soul.

24

DESPULLES l'aigua amb les mans, i apareix la set. Despulles la set amb la boca, i apareix la interrogació. Proves de seguir, proves de descordar la realitat botó a botó, de treure-li tota la roba fins a fregar la delícia lenta de la pell definitiva. Qui ha interposat tants vels en aquesta dansa? Facis el que facis, les mans ensopegaran amb roba, massa roba, tanta roba que et serà impossible saber què és cada cosa més enllà de la definició cansada del diccionari.

39

LA inèrcia és una estranya propietat de la matèria. Quan marxes, per exemple, l'aire conserva l'escalfor del teu cos durant una estona, així com la sorra guarda tota la nit la tebior trista del sol. Quan marxes, per continuar amb el mateix exemple, les meves mans persisteixen en la carícia, malgrat que ja no hi ha pell per acariciar, només la carcanada del record descomponent-se al buit de l'escala. Quan marxes, deixes enrere un *tu* invisible adherit a les coses més petites: potser un cabell a la coixinera, una mirada que s'ha entortolligat amb els tirants del desig, una crosteta de saliva a les comissures del sofà, una molècula de tendresa al plat de la dutxa. No és difícil trobar-te: l'amor em fa de lupa.

47

AMB les pinces metàl·liques de la intel·ligència, intentàrem llevar el color de la matèria, com qui lleva la membrana gelatinosa que recobreix els òrgans. Provàrem després d'extreure l'escalfor de cada granet de sorra – la paciència de l'un a un –, fins a obtenir un univers domèstic. Aïllar el pronom del verb, fins a deixar només l'os dur de l'infinitiu. Aïllar la bombolla del sabó, fins a deixar només la bellesa de l'esfera que s'envola. Aïllar el dolor del dolor, fins a deixar només el dolor.

58

LA felicitat s'assembla a un monosíl·lab. Per la seva senzillesa estructural. També, per la brevetat amb què ens visita la boca.

24

You strip water with your hands, and thirst appears. You strip thirst with your mouth, and the question appears. You try to follow, you try to unfasten reality button by button, to take off every bit of clothing until you stroke the slow delight of actual flesh. Who has interposed so many veils in this dance? Whatever you do, your hands will meet clothing, too much clothing, so much clothing you'll never be able to find out what each thing is beyond the tired meaning in the dictionary.

39

INERTIA is a strange property of matter. When you leave, for example, the air retains your body's warmth for a while, the way the sand retains all night the sad warmth of the sun. When you leave, to continue the same example, my hands persist in their caress, even though there is no skin to stroke, only the carcass of memory decomposing in the stairwell. When you leave, you leave behind an invisible *you* adhering to the smallest things: maybe a hair on the pillow, a glance tangled up with the strings of desire, a tiny crust of saliva in the creases of the sofa, a molecule of tenderness in the well of the shower. It isn't hard to find you: for me love works as a magnifying-glass.

47

WITH the metal tweezers of the mind, we attempted to lift the colour of matter, like one who lifts the gelatinous membrane covering the organs. We attempted afterwards to extract the heat from every grain of sand – the patience of the one-to-one – until we obtained a domestic universe. To isolate pronoun from verb, until we are left with the hard bone of the infinitive. To isolate the bubble from the soap until we are left with only the beauty of the sphere that floats away. To isolate pain from pain, until we are left with pain alone.

58

HAPPINESS is like a monosyllable. Because of its structural simplicity. And also because of the brevity with which it visits our mouths.

MANUEL FORCANO

PHOTO:AUTHOR'S ARCHIVE

MANUEL FORCANO (born Barcelona, 1968) has a PhD in Semitic Philology. He completed his studies in Israel, Syria and Egypt, and has worked as a lecturer in Hebrew and Aramaic at the University of Barcelona (1996-2004). He has translated literary works from Hebrew (Yehuda Amichai, Pinhas Sade, Ronny Someck, Amos Oz), Arabic (*The Travels of Ibn Battuta*), from French (Gabriele D'Annunzio's *Le Martyre de Saint Sébastien*, and the complete Catalan version of *The Travels of Marco Polo*), from English (*Pharos and Pharillon, an Evocation of Alexandria* by E. M. Forster), and Italian Baroque opera libretti. Published anthologies of his own poems include *Corint* (Corinth, winner of the Barcelona Jocs Florals Prize, 2000), *Com un persa* (Like a Persian, the Tivoli International Prize, 2002), *El tren de Bagdad* (The Baghdad Train, Carles Riba Prize, 2003), and *Llei d'estrangeria* (Law Governing Aliens, Qwerty Prize, 2008). He has worked as a researcher and playwright at the Jordi Savall Early Music International Centre Foundation since 2004.

* * *

Quan el vespre es va enfosquint,
tot s'enfonsa en llum que fuig.
Però els records
         – imatges teves clavades amb agulles
         rere els ulls –
brillen com l'alba
i el cos,
el cos és un gall cantant de nit
confós.

* * *

Al llit, quan ja no hi ha llum,
amb les mans
em tapo els ulls per no veure la nit.
I en aquest petit espai
que s'aixeca de les parpelles als palmells
creixen els somnis
com flors dins hivernacles.

* * *

El meu amor és
com el traç blanc d'un avió pel cel:
no sé d'on ve, no sé on va,
sóc passatger i pilot alhora.
Potser el cel, ample com és,
podrà capir-lo i guardar-lo dins un núvol,
perquè en el meu cor
només hi cap el polsim cremat
que els motors deixen
per l'aire.

* * *

Sempre és de nit
a dins del somni.
Sovint hi plou i bufa un vent

* * *

As dusk gathers and deepens,
everything disappears with the fleeing light.
But memories –
        pictures of you fixed with needles
        behind my eyes –
shine like the dawn
and the body,
the body is a cock singing by night
bewildered.

* * *

In bed, when the light is gone,
with my hands
I cover my eyes to blot out the night.
And in this tiny space
that's made between my eyelids and my palms
dreams grow
like flowers in a greenhouse.

* * *

My love is
like the white trail left by a plane in the sky:
I don't know where it comes from, or where it is going,
I am both passenger and pilot.
Perhaps the sky, broad as it is,
will comprehend it and keep it safe inside a cloud,
since in my heart
there is space only for the burnt dust
that the engines leave
in the air.

* * *

It is always night
inside the dream.
Often it's raining and a wind blows

que escampa arreu
llavors de bardissars i flors d'espines.

I per més que busco i miro
no puc entendre d'on cau aquesta pluja
sense núvols,
com si tot el món s'omplís, de sobte,
de nens orfes.

EL BOSC D'EFRAÏM
2 Samuel, 18:6-15

Ja hi has entrat algun altre cop. El camí
és ple de roses d'un urgent vermell de llavis.
Dins, sents la forta olor dels arbres com d'un cos
i n'has tastat els fruits madurs.

No hi vas sol, i t'hi endinses
sense fer cas, però, dels gestos recargolats
de les alzines que t'avisen de la branca
que finalment se t'enredarà als cabells
i quedaràs com Absalom
– entre cel i terra
penjat pel cap movent les cames –
agonitzant, un altre cop,
a l'obagor més sola.

TROMPE L'OEIL

No us cregueu massa tota aquesta tristor,
és com la llàgrima de maquillatge
a la cara d'un pallasso.

Però també malfieu-vos del gest fàcil i prim
que em fan els ulls i la boca en somriure:
només és l'alegria d'un cec
atrapat de sobte per la llum d'un raig de sol.

that scatters all around
the seeds of brambles and flowers with thorns.

And however much I search and stare
I cannot understand where it falls from, this rain
with never a cloud,
as though the whole world were suddenly filled
with orphaned children.

EPHRAIM'S WOOD

2 Samuel, 18:6-15

Once again you have entered it. The path
is thick with roses of an urgent red, like lips.
Within, you smell the strong scent of the trees like a body's
and you have tasted its ripe fruit.

You are not alone, and you go in further
paying no heed, however, to the twisting movements
of the oaks which warn you of the branch
which will finally catch in your hair
and you will be caught like Absalom –
between heaven and earth
hanging by your head but moving your legs –
in your death throes once again,
in the shade grown yet more lonely.

TROMPE L'OEIL

Don't place too much belief in all this sadness,
it's like the cosmetic tear
on the face of a clown.

But beware too of the thin and easy expression
a smile lends to eyes and mouth:
it is only the happiness of a blind man
suddenly caught in the light from a ray of sun.

TARD

Sovint arribem tard als records
i descobrim inconnexos per la memòria
besos com esqueixos de geranis vermells
que hem oblidat plantar.

De res serveix aleshores
refer el gest d'unes mans que hem estimat:
la desmemòria és un calaix obert
ple de guants desparionats.

DE NIT

Quan totes les formes d'amor
et semblin vanes.
Quan els records i la por. Quan el cos
tremoli, fràgil,
sorprès de la dolor que el té.
Quan aquesta foscor t'embeni fort els ulls,
aleshores,
vés i arriba't a les palpentes a la cuina
i a poc a poc
il·lumina-la amb la llum de la nevera:

mira, de sobte ets enmig d'un camp de flors
dibuixades pertot a les rajoles.

AL MUSEU ARQUEOLÒGIC DE DAMASC

Aquesta tarda, sol i en silenci,
vagarejant per la penombra
d'aquestes sales grans i altes de sostre,
t'he vist de sobte
en un cos sense mans de marbre nu,
com vaig deixar-te.
I he besat els teus llavis
d'estàtua.

Perquè som part de la mateixa runa.

LATE

We often come to recollections late,
and discover, disconnected by memory,
kisses like cuttings of red geraniums
we forgot to plant.

It's no use then
to recreate that gesture made by hands we loved:
forgetfulness is an open trunk
full of gloves, all odd.

AT NIGHT

When all forms of love
seem futile.
When memories and fear. When the body
shudders, vulnerable,
caught unawares by the pain it feels.
When this darkness tightly binds your eyes,
then,
see and grope your way to the kitchen
and little by little
illuminate it with the light from the fridge:

look, suddenly you're in the middle of a meadow full of flowers
drawn everywhere on the tiles.

AT THE ARCHAEOLOGICAL MUSEUM IN DAMASCUS

This afternoon, alone and in silence,
wandering through the twilight
of these vast, high-ceilinged rooms,
I suddenly saw you
in a marble statue with no hands and naked
as I left you.
And I kissed your statue's
lips.

Because we are part of the same rubble.

TREBIZONDA

T'esgoten els llargs camins dels teus amors imaginaris,
les pors que amb tot això arrossegues.
I vas com un soldat que recula i fuig
mal calçat per camps de neu:
cada passa se t'enfonsa profunda.
L'enemic que dus dins teu t'empaita
i et saps com mai
vulnerable.

Esperes, però,
el dia en què també tu de sobte
        – com els soldats de Xenofont
          per entre els cims gelats d'Armènia –
albiraràs, per fi,
la ciutat de Trebizonda:
una línia càlida de platja i la mar
al fons, tan blava.

EXILI

Quan t'afeixuga l'olor de terra endins i sents el mar
llunyíssim, quan s'apodera de tu
aquesta sensació enorme, sempre,
de fatiga,
seus al migdia i rellegeixes mig a l'ombra de la pèrgola
les sàtires que Juvenal va escriure a Assuan
en el seu dubtós exili a Egipte.

No t'interessa la crítica ferotge dels costums romans,
ni la descripció dels carrers bruts ni del brogit,
i et són indiferents els banquets i la gula del senador Emili Paulus
o els adulteris de la seva esposa Bíbula.

Tu només voldries cada cop que aixeques els ulls de la lectura
descobrir de sobte davant teu el seu mateix paisatge:
veure lliscar plàcidament el Nil, o seguir amb els ulls
el vol d'un ibis blanc fenent l'aire,
i així agrair també tu
els teus dies d'exili.

TREBIZOND

The long roads of your imaginary love affairs drain you,
the terrors you trail around with all that.
And you go like a soldier who retreats and flees
badly shod through fields of snow:
With every step you sink more deeply.
The enemy you carry within pursues you
and you know yourself to be vulnerable
as never before.

You are waiting, however,
for the day when you too, suddenly –
        like the soldiers of Xenophon
        among the frozen peaks of Armenia –
will glimpse, at last,
the city of Trebizond:
a warm line of beach and the sea
beyond, so blue.

EXILE

When the smell of the soil inland oppresses you and you feel how far away
the sea is, when you are overwhelmed
by this huge sensation that never leaves you,
of fatigue,
you sit down at midday and read again, half in the pergola's shade,
the satires that Juvenal wrote at Aswan
in his dubious exile in Egypt.

You're not interested in his fierce criticism of Roman customs,
or the description of the filthy streets or their din,
and you're indifferent to the banquets and gluttony of senator Emilius Paulus
or the adultery of his wife, Bibula.

The only thing you want, each time you raise your eyes from your book
is to find set out before you his same landscape:
to watch the Nile gliding placidly by, or to follow with your eyes
the flight of a white ibis cleaving the air,
and thus enjoy, you too,
your days of exile.

LA CASA DE PÍNDAR

Podem en la memòria,
com el darrer cop d'una destral al tronc d'un arbre,
convertir tots els records en un temps
que ja no reconeixerem mai més
com a nostre.

Però cal salvar-ne sempre alguna cosa:
la llum d'un vespre, el gest d'una carícia,
la calor brillant després d'un bes
als llavis.
      Com Alexandre amb Tebes:
va enderrocar pedra a pedra la ciutat hostil,
però hi deixà en peu
la casa de Píndar.

LES ROSES D'ISFAHAN

Les roses d'Isfahan, o de l'Eufrat
els lliris salvatges que creixien a les ribes.
Els jardins d'olor a Mossul, i a Damasc
l'esclat dels gessamins. Les flors de mirra del Sudan,
i a Khartum els dos grans afluents del Nil
arribant-se l'un a l'altre
com set i aigua, vaixell i port,
desig i cos.

No et conformis amb els geranis d'un test a la finestra.

POÈTICA

Heròdot conta que els perses van saquejar Atenes
i van robar les estàtues de tan belles com eren.
Les custodiaren en vergers frondosos als palaus de Sussa
i a Persèpolis, en castells al peu dels Zagres,
en mansions sumptuoses a la riba dels gran rius.

Talment com ells, camines per la ciutat
àvid de trobar la bellesa a què et deus

PINDAR'S HOUSE

In the mind we are able,
like an axe's final stroke in the trunk of a tree,
to change all memories of a time
that we'll no longer recognise any more
as our own.

But out of this one thing at least must be saved:
the light of a single evening, the gesture of a caress,
the brilliant heat that follows a kiss
on the lips.
        As Alexander did with Thebes:
he pulled down that hostile city, stone by stone,
but he left standing
Pindar's house.

THE ROSES OF ISFAHAN

The roses of Isfahan, or the wild iris
·that grow on the banks of the Euphrates.
The scented gardens at Mossul, and in Damascus
the dazzle of jasmine. The myrrh blossom of Sudan,
and at Khartoum the two huge tributaries of the Nile
rubbing shores one with the other
like thirst and water, vessel and port,
desire and flesh.

Don't be content with the pot of geraniums in the window.

POETICA

Herodotus recounts how the Persians sacked Athens
and stole the statues, so beautiful were they.
And they kept them safe in leafy orchards at the palaces of Sussa
and Persepolis, in castles a the foot of the Zagres,
in sumptuous mansions on the banks of the great rivers.

Like them, you walk through the city
eager to find that beauty to which you owe yourself

i fer-la teva: et meravella un rostre, el gest
d'unes mans, la forma entreoberta
d'uns llavis, el llambreig
d'uns ulls, l'amor possible, el goig
resposta del desig. I els atresores,
somniats, viscuts, a la memòria.

Sovint t'hi submergeixes com fan els buscadors de perles
al fons il·luminat de l'Índic, i emergeixes
a les mans plaers o restes de naufragi.
Perquè hi ha records de triomf que veneres
com els antics feien als temples
amb les figures dels déus, i els reses.

A voltes, però, el passat és una pica plena fins a dalt de plats,
de gots a mig beure i ganivets en punta.
I l'oblit és capriciós: conserva noses i pors,
corca i esborra aquells moments de joia.
I te'n manquen i vols restituir-los
i surts de casa com un antic guerrer prest al saqueig.
Com un persa.

ATEMPTAT

Com algú que a les fosques palpa una paret
fins a trobar l'interruptor,
et cerco a la memòria.
La llum sobtada del record
em regala de tu només fragments:
refer-los és caminar en un desert
cap a un miratge,
donar a la set
aigua de mar.
            L'oblit,
un fanàtic que mutila amb un martell
el cos nu d'una estàtua.

and make it your own: a face amazes you, the gesture
some hands make, the half-parted shape
of a pair of lips, the flash
of a pair of eyes, possible love, the joy
of answering desire. And you hoard them,
dreamed of, lived, in your memory.

Often you submerge yourself in them like pearl-fishers
in the illuminated depths of the Indian Ocean, and you surface
with hands full of pleasures or the remains of a shipwreck.
Because there are memories of triumph that you worship
as the ancients did in their temples
with the figures of the gods, and you pray to them.

Sometimes, though, the past is a sink piled high with dishes,
with half-drunk glasses and knives sticking up.
And forgetfulness is capricious: it keeps hindrances and fears,
it devours and wipes out those treasured moments.
And you miss them and want to restore them
and you leave your house like a warrior of old prepared for plunder.
Like a Persian.

ASSAULT

Like one who in the dark gropes along a wall
until he finds the switch,
I search for you in my mind's store.
The sudden light of memory
brings me only fragments of you:
piecing them together means walking in a desert
towards a mirage,
quenching thirst
with sea water.
          Oblivion,
a fanatic who mutilates with a hammer
a statue's marble body.

OMBRA MAI FU

> Ombra mai fu, di vegetabile cara
> ed amabile soave più
>
> (Mai l'ombra d'un arbre no fou / tan preciosa,amable i suau)
>
> *Serse*, de G. F. Handel

Recordar exacte un rosa besat de llavis
és provar d'encendre un foc
amb llumins que ja han cremat.
Però queden a la memòria
el mar resplendent des del camí,
l'ombra d'aquell arbre ufanós
on amb tot el cos a la veu vas dir-me vine.
Lluïa al sol el metall nu de les bicicletes a terra
l'una damunt de l'altra.

AL CAFÈ SÀHEL D'ALEP

> «Si no l'hagués abraçat, hauria gemegat fins al dia del Judici.»
>
> Dita del profeta Muhàmmad

Al cafè Sàhel d'Alep
els homes juguen a cartes:
passa pels seus dits la sort
com si palpessin per uns instants
la nuesa del cos que més cops han somniat.
Jo també la vaig tenir:
la teva pell
em besà els llavis,
i tot a l'engir meu
va ser canviant. Perquè un cos
pot arribar a canviar la història:
el jove Heliogàbal va ballar nu davant dels tòtems
i les legions de Síria el van fer emperador.
I Apià escriu a les *Guerres de Mitrídates*
que Menes, per emprendre la conquesta de Bitínia,
va convèncer dos mil soldats
mostrant-se en una arenga
nu. Perquè un cos
pot arribar a canviar la teva història:
ja era fosc. El muetzí acabava de cantar
la pregària de la nit. La cambra humil

OMBRA MAI FU

> Ombra mai fu, di vegetabile cara
> ed amabile soave più
>
> (Never was a tree's shade / more lovely, amiable and sweet)
> *Serse*, by G. F. Handel

To remember exactly the rosy kiss of lips
is to attempt to light a fire
with spent matches.
But there remain in the memory
the radiance of the sea seen from the path,
the shade of that luxuriant tree
where with your whole body in your voice you said to me
come here.
The bare metal of the bikes on the ground shone in the sun
one on top of another.

AT THE CAFÉ SAHEL IN ALEPPO

> "If you had not embraced him, you would have howled till Judgement Day."
> A saying of the prophet Mohammed

At the café Sahel in Aleppo
men play cards:
fate slips through their fingers
as though for a few instants they touched
the nakedness of the body they have most dreamed of.
I too have held this fate:
your skin
kissed my lips,
and everything around me
began to change. For a body
can succeed in changing history:
the young Heliogabalus danced naked before the totems
and the Syrian legions made him emperor.
And Appian writes in his *Wars of Mithridates*
that Menes, to undertake the conquest of Bithynia,
persuaded two thousand soldiers
by delivering a speech
naked. For a body
can succeed in changing your history:
it was now dark. The muezzin had just chanted
the night prayer. The modest room

d'aquell hotel al barri dels garatges
on els mecànics amb la boca
inflaven els pneumàtics, descargolaven tubs
i els regalimava a les mans
oli.

Al cafè Sàhel d'Alep
els homes tenen tot el temps del món:
per a ells el sol i la lluna
giren només al voltant dels asos.
Però tu i jo vam
estimar-nos només una setmana,
el temps exacte per convertir-nos
l'un en mans de l'altre
en runa. Igual com se saqueja
una ciutat: records de foc
i catapultes, de mans pels cossos
com escamots de soldats embogits
a mata-degolla pels carrers:
quina porta resisteix els cops de l'ariet?
No és només superfície,
la carícia.
Però la passió viscuda en temps tan breu
ens féu ser vaixell enamorat
del fons del mar, i ara ho recordo
com qui contempla emergir
lenta
l'última bombolla d'aire que surt d'un derelicte.

Al cafè Sàhel d'Alep
els homes fan trampes:
als plecs de les gel·labes amaguen cartes,
car saben que sovint la sort
s'amaga just sota la roba,
igual que sota la pell
el sucre de les fruites.
I fan un posat seriós i dissimulen
fins que guanyen. La victòria
és sempre nua: a l'estàtua
de la plaça de la Revolució d'Alep
els obrers alcen el puny des d'un cos nu de pedra,
i hom sap que els antics atletes
pujaven al pòdium despullats.
Tu i jo cercàvem aquest triomf

in that hotel in the district full of garages
where mechanics inflated tyres
with their mouths, uncoiled piping
and ended up with their hands dripping
with oil.

At the café Sahel in Aleppo
the men have all the time in the world:
for them the sun and the moon
turn only round aces.
But you and I
we loved each other for only a week,
just the time it took to turn us,
the one in the hands of the other,
into rubble. The way you would sack
a city: memories of fire
and catapults, of hands upon bodies
like squads of maddened soldiers
at daggers drawn in the streets:
what door can withstand the blows of a battering-ram?
It's not only on the surface,
caressing.
But passion lived in so short a time
made of us a vessel in love
with the bottom of the sea, and I remember it now
as one who contemplates the slow
surfacing
of the final bubble of air rising up from a wreck.

At the café Sahel in Aleppo
the men cheat:
they conceal cards in the folds of their djellabas,
for they know that fate often
hides just beneath a garment,
just as under the skin
fruits have their juice.
And they strike a serious pose and dissemble
until they win. Victory
is always naked: on the statue
in Revolution Square in Aleppo
workers raise fists from a naked body made of stone,
and we know that in ancient times athletes
wore no clothing when they climbed the podium.
You and I sought this triumph

i amb les testes coronades de llorer
l'haguérem. Ara
al mirall cerco rastres als meus llavis
dels teus, però no roman sempre a la branca
la flor roja del festuc,
ni l'ocell del teu tacte
en la gàbia de la meva pell.
Res del que ocupa una gàbia sobreviu,
tampoc res del que no n'ocupa cap
i al cafè Sàhel d'Alep
els homes fan brega i amb veu forta criden
quan descobreixen el trampós.

Al cafè Sàhel d'Alep, quan plou,
els homes deixen les cartes.
Miren la pluja i aposten quin cotxe
sortirà primer del tap de trànsit a baix a la cruïlla:
el Nissan blau, el Peugeot blanc,
el carro de les síndries,
o el taxi groc on tu i jo anàvem
cap a la ciutadella:
mira la runa oberta i satisfeta,
car les muralles volen que les penetri
l'enemic. El desig
sempre fa cedir les baldes
i la mola inexpugnable riu
quan l'exèrcit contrari l'envaeix:
els amants s'enfonsen l'un dins l'altre
com una cullera en un plat calent de sopa.
Des de la runa d'una torre
vam contemplar la ciutat sota la pluja:
«El teu cos té just l'amplada
de l'abraçada que somnio», vaig dir,
i sense cap mà que l'agafés
el paraigua va envolar-se.

Al cafè Sàhel d'Alep
els homes fumen pipes d'aigua:
crema el tabac de mel o poma
i de la boca els surt un arabesc de fum.
A cada pipada el narguil bull
com jo al tacte d'aquells besos
que amb la pressa del desig
em malreparties pel cos

and with our brows crowned with laurel
we had it. Now
I search the mirror for traces of your lips
on mine, but it doesn't remain on the branch forever,
the red pistachio flower,
nor the bird of your touch
in the cage of my skin.
Nothing that stays in a cage survives,
nor yet anything that doesn't,
and at the café Sahel in Aleppo
the men quarrel and shout at the top of their voices
when they discover the cheat.

At the café Sahel in Aleppo, when it rains,
the men lay down their cards.
They watch the rain and lay bets as to which car
will exit the traffic bottle-neck first below the junction:
the blue Nissan, the white Peugeot,
the watermelon cart,
or the yellow taxi that you and I used to take
up to the citadel:
look at the rubble lying open and satisfied,
for walls want the enemy
to penetrate them. Desire
always makes the bolts give way
and the unyielding mass laughs
when the opposing army breaks through:
lovers plunge one into another
like a spoon into a plate of hot soup.
From the rubble of a tower
we gazed down on the city in the rain:
"Your body has just the breadth
of the embrace I dream of," I said,
and with no hand to hold it
the umbrella flew away.

At the café Sahel in Aleppo
the men smoke hookahs:
the honey- or apple-scented tobacco burns
and from the mouth there rises an arabesque of smoke.
With every indrawn breath the narguile boils
as I did under the touch of those kisses
that in the rush of desire
you showered unequably over my body

mentre jo feia per entendre
l'alegria de l'imant i el ferro
quan s'enganxen.
Però al mar,
de nit,
l'escuma també és negra,
i ara sé l'amor
un escampall de pètals
caiguts del ram collit ahir.
Tot s'esvaeix, com aquest fum
entre les aspes lentes dels ventiladors
damunt els jugadors de cartes,
i la brasa de la pipa perd el foc,
els crepits callen:
es marfonen els records
com si a poc a poc ens tornéssim cecs
per dins. Només els colors
no deixen mai de ser-ho.

Al cafè Sàhel d'Alep
els homes beuen amb destresa el te d'hibiscus
sense gairebé mullar-se els llavis.
Quan ja no hi eres
als vespres sortia a trobar-te
als llavis que la meva boca
besaria. Hores pel basar
cercant en quin altre cos
podria haver-te:
al carrer dels perfumistes,
¿en l'olor de quin arbre talat
o de la mort de quines flors
t'hauria?
A la soc dels treballadors del coure,
creia veure't a les guspires
que saltaven dels cops dels seus martells.
I al carrer dels carnissers, finalment,
vaig abraçar un be escorxat penjat d'un garfi
car res d'altre no s'assemblava més
a la nuesa extrema que vam dar-nos:
aquell tacte calent i humit,
el cor a la vista
i la sang rient pertot arreu.
Perdura insolent el desig:
sempre tenen set els gots.

while I tried to understand
the delight of magnet and iron
when they come together.
But in the sea
at night
the foam too is black,
and now I know love
to be a scattering of petals
fallen from the bouquet picked yesterday.
Everything vanishes, like this smoke
between the blades of the ceiling-fans
above the card players,
and the pipe's embers die,
the cracklings fall silent:
memories waste away
as though we were slowly to grow blind
within. Only colours
never stop being themselves.

At the café Sahel in Aleppo
the men drink their hibiscus tea adroitly
almost without wetting their lips.
When you were no longer here
I'd go out evenings to find you
in lips that my mouth
would kiss. For hours through the bazaar
searching to see in what other body
I might possess you:
in the street of the perfume-makers,
in the scent of what felled tree
or out of the death of what flowers
might I possess you?
In the souk of the coppersmiths,
I thought I glimpsed you in the sparks
that leapt from their hammer blows.
And in the street of the butchers, in the end,
I embraced a flayed sheep hanging from a hook
for nothing else resembled more
the utter nakedness that we gave each other:
that hot, damp touch,
the heart visible
and the blood laughing all around.
Desire remains, insolent:
the vessels are always thirsty.

Al cafè Sàhel d'Alep
els homes no obliden mai a qui toca escapçar
o repartir les cartes. Tampoc jo
aquells dies de sol,
taronja oberta
i a l'entorn dels llavis i als dits
suc. De tu,
torno a ser cel que enyora ales volant-lo.
Et penso enlluernat
igual com es camina amb sol de cara.
I et recordo com els cecs
que al pati de la gran mesquita
reciten per una almoina
la sura de la Llum de l'Alcorà.
Els dono una moneda
que no val la claror que ja no veuen
ni tampoc en mi
la teva absència.
Hi ha moltes formes de pobresa,
però al cafè Sàhel d'Alep
els homes no tornen mai a casa
si perden la partida:
juguen una altra timba.
Fins que guanyen.

PER FI

Somniar ser vi.
Sentir-se raïm madur.

I veure atansar-se el veremador,
per fi.

LLEI D'ESTRANGERIA

El meu país és el desig
que em fa anar a l'estranger de mi.

Sóc sempre emigrant al cor d'algú:
li aprenc l'idioma,

At the café Sahel in Aleppo
the men never forget whose turn it is to cut
or to deal the cards. I too
those days of sun,
an orange cut open
and juice around lips
and fingers. For you,
I go back to being sky missing wings flying through it.
I think of you dazzled
like walking with the sun in your face.
I remember you as the blind men
who in the courtyard of the mosque
recite for a gift of alms
the *surah of Light* from the Koran.
I give them a coin
that is not worth the brightness they no longer see
nor in me
your absence.
Poverty takes many forms,
but at the café Sahel in Aleppo
the men never go home
if they lose a game:
they play in another gaming-house.
Until they win.

AT LAST

A dream of being wine.
Feeling yourself to be a grape, and ripe.

And seeing the vintager approaching,
at last.

LAW GOVERNING ALIENS

My country is desire
which makes me go to the foreign country of myself.

I am always an emigrant in someone's heart:
I learn his language,

el clima, el cos,
menjo el que hi ha,
allò que em donen.

Fins que,
      llei en mà,
           m'expulsen
o jo surto a cercar nous horitzons.
Mans invisibles ens empenyen.

No sé si prospero.
Sobrevisc.

CALL

Caminava distret pel Call
i els peus van dur-me fins a un immoble
on fa uns quanta anys vaig estimar algú.

Carrer Marlet, quart pis, just dessota el terrat.
Aquella cambra ampla.
Aquells besos dats amb pressa
perquè la nit se'ns feia curta.
Perquè l'amor se'ns va fer curt.

Ara veig paletes que hi treballen.
Restauren l'edifici.
Hi fan un museu – em diuen –
sobre la història dels jueus.

Jo sé que quan el visiti
cercaré aquella cambra del quart pis,
la reconeixeré,
i davant els panells explicatius
de la ruïna de Jerusalem
i davant les fotos d'Auschwitz
ploraré.

climate, body,
I eat what there is,
what they give me.

Until,
        law in hand,
                    they expel me
or I go out to search for new horizons.
Invisible hands push us.

I don't know whether I prosper.
I survive.

WALKING THROUGH THE CALL*

I was walking absentmindedly through the Call
and my feet led me to a building
where some years ago I loved someone.

Marlet Street, fourth floor, just below the terrace roof.
That spacious room.
Those kisses given in haste
because the night was running out for us.
Because love ran out for us.

Now I see bricklayers working there.
They are restoring the building.
They are creating a museum – so they tell me –
about the history of the Jews.

I know that when I visit it
I will search for that fourth-floor room,
I'll recognise it,
and by the interpretation-boards
about the fall of Jerusalem
and by the photos of Auschwitz
I will weep.

* The Call is the old Jewish quarter.

JOSEP LLUÍS AGUILÓ

Josep Lluís Aguiló (born Manacor, Mallorca, 1967), poet and businessman, works as a marketing and advertising director.

In 1986 he published his first collection of poems, *Cants d'Arjau* (Songs from the Helm), which he wrote when he was between sixteen and eighteen years of age. After an interval of eighteen years, he published two further collections, *La biblioteca secreta* (The Secret Library) and *L'estació de les ombres* (Season of Shadows), both in 2004.

His collection *Monstres* (Monsters, 2005) was awarded the Premi Ciutat de Palma Joan Alcocer Poetry Prize in 2005 and, in 2006, the National Critics' Prize for the best book of poems written in Catalan, while it also received a special mention from the jury of the Critics' Prizes for Catalan Writers. In 2007, the Manacor School of Mallorcan Language gave him its Recognition of Merits Award for his work in writing Catalan poetry and helping to make it better known. The University of the Balearic Islands has published his collection *Antologia Personal* (Personal Anthology).

In 2008, Josep Lluís Aguiló was the winner of the literary competition Jocs Florals de Barcelona with his work *Llunari* (Calendar). His writings have appeared in several anthologies and have been translated into a number of languages.

CANTS D'ARJAU, XII

La quietud de l'horabaixa es fa ple de lluna
i l'àmbit dels plaers un record boirós.
Quan la taula d'ònix vetat delimita nostra unió,
asseguts, enfront.
Escolta això, Heura: el brau grata en terra
(furiosa delectança)
tant quan va a envestir com a estimar.
Tots tenim alguna cosa de brau,
alguns només el desig.

LA BIBLIOTECA SECRETA

Com els traços de la tinta que defineixen
el temps ocult, les temibles ratlles dels tigres
i els jeroglífics de les taques del jaguar
mostren l'escriptura d'un déu afeccionat
als astuts felins d'or i a la seva gràcia.

Al Puig de Randa, a Mallorca, Ramon Llull
desxifrava a les fulles de la *mata escrita*
cada dia les paraules verdes i grogues
dels capítols escrits per un déu botànic.

Se'ns ha revelat que el que busquem ens espera
als llibres muts d'una biblioteca secreta.

Podem començar a cercar la veritat
trobant on s'amaga la tinta que ens tatua
al món; l'escriptura breu d'esteles que ens ha
descrit a l'oceà. A la batalla que ens ha
estat promesa, al lloc d'avantguarda a què
se'ns destina abans de l'atac de l'enemic
o dins dels arxius d'un bibliotecari cec
trobarem les portes d'or, els panys i les claus
de la biblioteca secreta de l'oblit.

SONGS FROM THE HELM, XII

The calm of dusk becomes full moon
and the boundary of pleasures a blurred memory.
When the table of veined onyx limits our coming together,
sitting, facing each other.
Listen to this, Heura: the bull paws at the ground
(furious delight)
as much when it is going to attack as when it prepares for love.
We all share something of the bull,
while some have only desire.

THE SECRET LIBRARY

Like the traces of ink that define
hidden ages, the fearsome stripes of tigers
and the hieroglyphics of the jaguar's markings
show the writing of a god well-disposed
to clever golden felines and their grace.

At Puig de Randa, in Mallorca, Ramon Llull
deciphered every day on the pages of
the *thicket of writing* the green and yellow words
of chapters written by a botanical god.

It has been revealed that what we are searching for awaits us
in the dumb books of a secret library.

We can begin to search for the truth
by finding where the ink is hidden that tattoos us
in the world: the scant writing of stars that has
described us in the ocean. In the battle that has
been promised us, at the place at the front to which
we are destined before the attack by the enemy
or in the archives of a blind librarian
we will find the golden doors, the locks and the keys
of oblivion's secret library.

ELS PONTS DEL DIABLE

El dimoni construeix ponts i després
en demana la paga. Els que li han manat la feina,
invariablement més espavilats, sempre l'enganyen.

Sempre demana que li deixin endur-se'n
l'últim o el primer que passarà pel pont.
Si ha demanat que li regalin l'últim
el darrer que passa li diu: «agafa aquest»,
senyalant, sorneguer, la seva ombra.

Si ha demanat el primer fan passar-hi un animal.
Sovint és un moix o un gall, els cans
són massa de la família com per regalar-los
a algú, per molt diable que sigui.

No n'aprèn. Em deman què en fa de la col·lecció
d'ombres i de bèsties. Segurament res.

El dimoni, sense dubte, frueix fent ponts.
Els cavallers tenen aficions xocants;
embotellar vaixells, pintar aquarel·les,
escriure memorials de greuges,
caçar. Quan s'avorreix ve i fa un pont
i dóna per parlar d'ell a generacions
que es vantaran de com la seva avior
no va saber res d'obres hidràuliques
però sí d'ensarronar diables.

PARAL·LELISMES

És ben bé una malaltia curiosa
la de cercar sempre paral·lelismes.
Podem començar per qualsevol cosa:

Matança dels innocents; ben curiós,
ja la trobem a Egipte, el Faraó
massacra els nounats, es salva Moisès.

Anys després Herodes també dedica
el temps a exterminar tots els nascuts
per mor d'assassinar un altre rei.

THE DEVIL'S BRIDGES

The devil builds bridges and afterwards
demands payment for them. Those who carried out the work,
invariably more wide-awake, always outwit him.

He always demands that he should carry off
the first or the last to cross the bridge.
If he has asked to be given the last one
then the final one to cross says to him, "grab this,"
pointing, cunningly, at his shadow.

If he has demanded the first, they let an animal cross over to him.
Often it's a cat or a cock, a dog
is too much a part of the family to be given away
to anyone, however much of a devil it might be.

He never learns, I wonder what he does with his collection
of shadows and beasts. Probably nothing.

The devil, no doubt, enjoys building bridges.
Swindlers have shocking hobbies:
putting ships into bottles, painting watercolours,
writing chronicles of wrongs done,
hunting. When one gets bored he comes and builds a bridge
and considers speaking about himself to generations
who will boast of how their ancestry
knew nothing of hydraulic works
but a lot about swindling devils.

PARALLELISMS

It certainly is a strange disease
this constantly searching for parallels.
We can begin with anything:

Slaughter of the innocents; very strange,
we already find it in Egypt, Pharaoh
massacres the newborn, Moses escapes.

Years later Herod too dedicates
his time to exterminating all the firstborn
in his longing to assassinate another king.

La història es torna a repetir
a la llegenda d'Artús de Bretanya
quan per matar el seu fill Mòrdred va fer
degollar tots els infants del seu regne.

No ens parem aquí. Seguirem el fil.

Als Anys Obscurs descobrim també hàbits
estranys en el disseny de fonaments
per ponts, esglésies i fortaleses.

A les murades de Höxter, a Vestemberg,
a l'església de Vilmnitz, a Germània,
hi ha cambres ocultes als fonaments
on hi enterraren infants comprats
per ben poc preu a les seves mares
per enfortir la construcció amb sang.

Deixau-me enllaçar-hi una altra història:

Any mil dos-cents dotze. Per tot Europa
avancen grups de nins. Es dirigeixen
a Marsella per embarcar a Terra
Santa i alliberar Jerusalem.

No hi ha notícia de qui els ha
ficat aquesta quimera al cap.
El gremi de mercaders de Marsella
organitza la flota i després
de grans tempestes i calamitats
es venen els nins a Tunis i el Caire.

Poc temps després naixeran les històries.

Devers l'any mil dos-cents vuitanta-quatre.
A la vila de Hameln. Segons consta
als papers del poble; un caçador
de rates, després de no ser pagat,
se'n du tots els infants de la ciutat.

Diuen alguns que els ha dut fins al riu.
D'altres diuen que sota una muntanya.
Alguns ens parlen de Constantinoble
i els seus famosos mercaders d'esclaus.

History repeats itself again
in the legend of Arthur of Britain
who, in order to kill his son Mordred, had
the throats of all the infants in his kingdom cut.

Let's not pause here. Let's follow the thread.

In the Dark Ages we discover strange
customs in the design of foundations
for bridges, churches and fortresses.

In the walls of Höxter, in Vestemberg,
in the church of Vilmnitz, in Germany,
there are chambers hidden in the foundations
where they buried children bought
at a very low price from their mothers
to strengthen the building with blood.

Allow me to weave in another story:

One thousand two hundred and twelve. All over Europe
groups of children are on the march. They make their way
to Marseilles to embark for the Holy
Land and liberate Jerusalem.

There is no record of who has
planted this chimera in their heads.
The guild of merchants in Marseilles
organizes the fleet and after
great storms and calamities
the children come to Tunis and Cairo.

Shortly afterwards the stories will start to appear.

Around twelve eighty-four.
In the town of Hamelin. According to
the town archives; a rat-
catcher, after failing to be paid,
lures away all the children in the town.

Some say he led them into the river.
Other say under a mountain.
Some talk of Constantinople
and its famous slave-markets.

Els imperis, com es veu, s'alimenten
de la mort dels infants i es basteixen
sobre els fonaments del seu sacrifici.

Els escura-xemeneies d'Anglaterra
adquirint el seu càncer de testicles
abans de la pubertat. Els miners
diminuts. Tot això ens recorda d'altres
històries. Podem afegir noms
de lloc. No ens fa falta la data exacta.
Congo Belga, Auschwitz, Vukovar, Mostar,
Serra Lleona, Thailandia, Iraq.

Basta. Traieu-ne les conclusions.

L'ESTACIÓ DE LES OMBRES

No viuré a l'estiu cremat
ni a la tardor marró ni a l'hivern gris
ni a una primavera tenyida de porpra imperial.
La meva estació és l'estació de les ombres,
temps de magranes i de raïm
de pluges desfetes i d'adéus i fins-a-un-altres.

Aquesta estació té la música impossible
d'Edith Piaf cantant Jacques Brel
i les llums només il·luminen mitja cara
a la gent que hi habita per un temps breu.

Les barques tornen carregades de peix
servioles i llampuga i alguna tonyina perduda
i la sang dibuixa vermells a la coberta dels llaüts.

A les biblioteques només hi ha atles
i gruixuts tractats de botànica.
A les parets emblanquinades
no hi ha quadres ni fotos, sols mapes.

No es parla gaire a l'estació de les ombres.
Les veus es difuminen fins que arriba el silenci
i no hi ha tinta per embalsamar les paraules.

Empires, as we can see, feed upon
the death of small children and are built
on the foundations of their sacrifice.

English chimney-sweeps
acquired their testicular cancer
before puberty. Stunted
miners. All this reminds us of other
stories. We can attach place-
names. There is no shortage of precise data.
Belgian Congo, Auschwitz, Vukovar, Mostar,
Sierra Leone, Thailand, Iraq.

Enough. Draw your own conclusions.

THE SEASON OF SHADOWS

I shall not live in scorched summer
nor in chestnut autumn or grey winter
nor in a spring dyed with imperial purple.
My season is the season of shadows,
a time of grapes and pomegranates
of torrential rain and farewells and bye-for-nows.

This season has the impossible music
of Edith Piaf singing Jacques Brel
and lamps light up only half the face
of people who live there for a short while.

The boats come in laden with fish
catheads and chrysophry and the odd strayed tunny
and blood paints its reds on the decks of the *llaüts**.

In the libraries there are only atlases
and thick treatises on botany.
On the whitewashed walls
there are no paintings or photos, only maps.

Hardly anyone speaks in the season of shadows.
Voices become diffused until there is only silence
and there is no ink to embalm words.

* *llaüts*: wooden fishing-boats, peculiar to Catalonia.

PARAULES

Solia dormir amb un quadern
a la taula de nit. Si es despertava
escrivia alguna paraula
per recordar l'endemà
el contingut dels somnis.

Al matí, quan es llevava, veia
que havia escrit paraules
com *terra, arròs, cornucòpia* o *compàs*.

Tot el que havia estat clar s'esvania
i enyorava l'instant de claredat
on tot es conjugava en un terme
i una paraula sola era sinònima de l'univers.

LUZBEL

Fa anys vaig caminar per sobre les roques
en un capvespre de juny. Els peus, punxats
per la sal dels cocons, patien un martiri
blanc. Les gavines bussejaven un esbart
de peix terroritzat. El sol, que només és sol en juny,
cremava despietat tot el verd del rocam.

Era un element de la comèdia. M'enfilava
amb la lleugeresa del dolor. Cada cama
suportava la meitat de la meitat
del meu pes d'al·lot ennegrit de juny.

Cada passa m'acostava al cim
d'un turó de sal i fonoll marí,
un claper de gegant que augmentava
el penya-segat menjat per tantes ones
d'aquella mar que m'esperava.
Al cim em vaig acostar a la vorera
disposat al salt definitiu, a la capbussada
en una verdor de mar sembrada d'algues.

Sentia ja la frescor anticipada, el vertigen marró
de les pedres que lleneguen davant dels ulls
i l'impacte amb la mar de duresa blava.

WORDS

He used to sleep with a notebook
on the bedside table. If he woke up
he would write down some word or other
that would remind him next day
of the content of his dreams.

In the morning, when he got up, he saw
that he had written words
such as *earth, rice, cornucopia* or *rhythm*.

Everything that had been clear vanished
and he yearned for the instant of clarity
when everything combined in a single term
and one word was synonymous with the universe.

LUCIFER

Years ago I went for a walk over the rocks
on a June evening. My feet, stung
by the brine of the rock-pools, suffered
a white martyrdom. The gulls were stabbing a terrorized
shoal of fish. The sun, which is the sun only in June,
was scorching without mercy the seaweed on the rocks.

I was one element in the comedy. I ran
with the lightness of the pain. Each leg
supported half of the half
of the weight of a sunburnt lad in June.

Every step brought me closer to the summit
of a hill of salt and sea-fennel,
a giant's pile of pebbles that added to
the height of the cliff devoured by so many waves
of that sea that was waiting for me.
At the summit I approached the edge
ready for the ultimate leap, for diving
into a greenness of sea sown with weed.

Already I felt the anticipated freshness, the brown dizziness
of the stones that slid before my eyes
and the impact of that sea with its blue hardness.

Vaig saltar, en una explosió de meravella
i el camí al blau es va fer etern, els ulls
desorbitats i la boca sense alens.

Baixant a la mar de juny era un àngel sense ales;
Luzbel que tornava al cel amb salconduit.

EL SÒTIL

Havia d'anar amb compte. Cada passa ressonava
amb renou de buit i de temps. Les olors de menjar
de la cuina no arribaven tan amunt i jo gratava
entre andròmines i roba vella, assaborint les olors
del segó de les gallines i els fems i les parets humides
de cantó de Santanyí i mal ciment mallorquí.
Hi havia senalles de bova amb el cul foradat
i les decoracions de molts nadals en una discreta tenebra.

El sòtil era un petit món, jo el visitava d'amagat
per viure lluny del terra i les advertències dels majors.
La terra prohibida on hi havia els diaris d'anys
i una biblioteca groga de missals i *Anys Cristians*.

També hi havia els trofeus del padrí desconegut;
un cascavell de serp, un ou d'estruç, una armadura
d'armadillo, óssos innominats, restes d'un bestiari
fantàstic arribat de més enllà de la mar.

Molts dies, encara ara d'amagat, m'enfil al sòtil.
M'assec a un racó, amb els ulls tancats, ensum
la sentor de molsa, fems de gallina i bova vella.
Llegesc, gairebé sense llum, amb les mans tenyides
de pols groga, papers menjats per l'arna i peixos de plata.

I m'oblid que ja fa uns quants anys que l'esbucàrem.

I jumped, in an explosion of wonder
and the blue path became forever, my eyes
starting from their sockets and no breath in my mouth.

Falling into the June sea I was an angel with no wings;
Lucifer re-entering heaven with a passport made of salt.

THE ATTIC

You had to walk stealthily. Every footstep echoed,
disturbing emptiness and time. The smells of food
from the kitchen did not reach this high and I scrabbled
among lumber and old clothes, savouring the smells
of chicken bran and the dung and damp walls
of this corner of Santanyí and bad Mallorcan cement.
There were baskets made from bulrushes, bottoms stove-in,
and decorations from many Christmases in a tactful gloom.

The attic was a little world, and I visited it secretly
so as to be far from the land and advice of the grown-ups.
The forbidden land where there were newspapers from years ago
and a yellow library of missals and *The Christian Year*.

There were also the trophies of an unknown godfather:
the rattle of a rattlesnake, an ostrich egg, the shell
of an armadillo, nameless bones, the remains of a fantastic
bestiary washed-up from across the seas.

Many days, still in secret now, I sneak up to the attic.
I sit in a corner, with my eyes closed, breathe in
the scent of moss, chicken-shit and old rushes.
With hardly any light, my hands stained by yellow dust,
I read papers eaten by moth and by silverfish.

And I forget that it's years since we demolished it.

MINOTAURE

La meva mare va embogir d'amor
per un brau blanc. Dèdal li va cosir
una eròtica disfressa de vaca.

El meu pare, Minos, va dir a Dèdal
que em fes un gran palau: amb passadissos
cecs, amb els camins entortolligats
i les sales i cambres amagades.

A cada paret hi va fer posar
un mirall per repetir la cadència;
el ritme detestable de la bèstia.
M'avesaren a tastar carn i sang
i a viure clos en un mausoleu cíclic.

Jo era el fill i el monstre i tots sabem bé
que els monstres s'enduen la pitjor part
del joc dels averanys i dels profetes.

El cap de brau és només una anècdota.
La meva part pitjor és la part d'home.

L'HOLANDÈS ERRANT

En una mar d'ones de dièsel
el meu vaixell segueix les esteles
monstruoses dels portacontenidors.
La meva tripulació fantasma
mai celebra el pas de l'equador
i s'engata amb un *grog* eteri
fet de records de llimones
i de focs de Sant Telm.

Un cop cada set anys davall a terra
per saber que encara és de veres,
que no és l'ombra d'una ombra.
Davall a platges d'Àfrica
o als ports on flamejaven les veles
dels vaixells insolents i on ara regnen
els esquelets repelats de les grues.

MINOTAUR

My mother went out of her mind with love
for a white bull. Daedalus sewed her
an erotic cow costume.

Minos, my father, told Daedalus
to build me a great palace: with blind
passages, with twisting paths
and concealed halls and rooms.

On every wall he had a mirror
placed to repeat the cadence;
the beast's detestable rhythm.
They accustomed me to tasting flesh and blood
and to live shut up in a cyclical mausoleum.

I was son and monster and we all know
that monsters play the worst part
in the game of omens and prophets.

The bull's head is just a story.
My worst part is the man's part.

THE FLYING DUTCHMAN

In a sea of diesel waves
my vessel follows the monstrous
stars of the container-ships.
My ghostly crew
never celebrates crossing the equator
and gets drunk on ethereal grog,
composed of memories of lemons
and of St Elmo's Fire.

Once every seven years I make landfall
just to know that it is really there,
that it's not just the shadow of a shadow.
I land on African beaches
or in ports where once there flamed the sails
of insolent ships and where now there dominate
the spindly skeletons of cranes.

I vull anotar en el llibre de bord
que els vaixells no canvien de càrrega
i que encara porten sedes, or i esclaus
en les bodegues de la memòria.

Si no fos perquè, cada set anys,
davall a terra i vaig a una cafeteria
del moll i parl amb la gent
del temps, que ja no es pesca
com abans, de les noies, de la hipoteca
que els espera a casa com una dalla,
de l'última tempesta que semblava sobrenatural,
de l'huracà que enfonsà tantes barques,
no creuria que la condemna és lleu
i que no estic fet per cap tomba a terra.
La terra és un parany.
No pot esser navegada com necessiten
navegar els cadàvers, sense rumb.
Pens que a Déu li plau l'orgull
i decidesc, per set anys més,
que no arrumbaré al sud
per por d'acostar-me, per accident,
al Cap de Bona Esperança.

HE PERDUT ALGUNS VERSOS

> «L'àngel de la canalla
> vindrà de grat amb una
> delegació dels seus.»
>
> Bartomeu Fiol, *Canalla lluny de Grècia*

Són com animals esquius,
a cops se'm passegen per sobre
o se m'esmunyen entre els peus
i em fan ensopegar.

N'he caçat sovint en l'última revinglada,
en els moviments més convulsos de l'amor;
després, endormiscat, he mig obert la mà
i han escapat d'entre els dits, com insectes.

També n'he perdut per mandra
de llevar-me del llit;

And I want to note in the ship's log
that the ships don't change their cargoes
and that they still carry silks, gold and slaves
in memory's holds.

If it weren't for the fact that, every seven years,
I go ashore and I go to a harbour café
and I talk to people
about the weather, for the fishing
is not what it was, about girls, and the mortgage
that waits for them at home like a millstone,
about the last storm that seemed supernatural,
about the hurricane that sank so many boats,
I would not believe that the sentence is light
and that I am not made for a grave on land.
The land is a trap.
It cannot be navigated as corpses
need to navigate, without steering.
I think that God admires pride
and I decide, for another seven years,
that I will not steer for the south
for fear of approaching, by mistake
the Cape of Good Hope.

I HAVE LOST A FEW LINES

> "The angel of the mob
> will willingly come with a
> delegation of his own."
>
> Bartolomeu Fiol, *The mob a long way from Greece*

They are like shy animals,
sometimes they pass right over me
or glide between my feet
and trip me up.

I have often chased them in the final spasm,
in the most convulsive movements of love-making;
later, dozing, I have half-opened my hand
and they escaped from between my fingers, like insects.

Some I have lost through idleness,
failing to get up from my bed;

si els enganxo a un paper
sovint acaben diluïts
en el sabó de la bugada.

O els ha espatllat l'esperit d'un licor,
una visita que venia de Porlock,
la urgència de l'últim cigarret
o els viatges imprevists al banc.

A moments em pensava
que la memòria, l'amant voluble
que no pot evitar trair-me,
els subjectava i no els deixava anar.

Com sempre, m'equivocava,
descurada com és, els va deixar
a l'abast de l'oblit.

El pitjor és que sóc conscient
que els versos fugitius
se'n van a un poema que rellegeixo
sovint al mig de la nit, i que no puc recordar
quan em treu del llit, amb la llum de l'alba,
la bóta de ferro del dia.

TUMBLEWEED

«Quantos Césares fui!»
    Fernando Pessoa-Álvaro de Campos, *Pecado Original*

Les seves mans esperen als revòlvers.
No deixa cap ombra el sol del migdia.

L'enemic està només a vint passes.
La imatge del duel es repeteix:
és l'enèsim encontre de la mà
amb el ferro modelat, per enèsima
vegada, amb una de les formes noves
que l'enginy ens permet donar a la mort.

La pols del carrer els ha cobert les botes,
els espectadors esperen el tret,
el saloon ha despatxat esperit
de fusta mesclat amb verí de serp.

if I pin them down on paper
they often end up diluted
by the soap in the washing-machine.

Or some spirituous liquor has ruined them,
or the visitor from Porlock,
or the need for a last cigarette
or unforeseen trips to the bank.

At times I have thought
that memory, that voluble lover
that cannot help but betray me,
was holding them and would not let them go.

As ever, I was wrong,
for being careless, she had left them
where oblivion could reach them.

The worst of it is, I'm aware
that those fugitive lines
went into a poem I read again
often in the middle of the night, a poem I can't recall
when I'm kicked out of bed, with the light of dawn,
by the iron boot of day.

TUMBLEWEED

"I was so many Caesars!"
Fernando Pessoa-Álvaro de Campos, *Original Sin*

Their hands await their revolvers.
The midday sun casts no shadow.

The enemy is only twenty paces away.
The image of the duel repeats itself:
it is the umpteenth meeting between hand
and pressed metal, for the umpteenth
time, with one of the new shapes
that ingenuity allows us to give death.

The dust of the street has covered their boots,
the spectators are waiting for the shot,
the saloon has sold liquor made from
wood mixed with snake-poison.

Fa sols tres dies que cavalquen junts.
Ara fa mesos que no s'han banyat.
Fa tres dies que esperen el moment
de l'explosió que alliberarà
una bala del seu catau de bronze.

Un d'ells porta al coll un amulet indi
(com és que el té és una altra història).
Un no ha matat mai ningú per l'esquena.
Un, mai no s'ha sentit tan viu com ara.

Un d'ells va deixar una dona i dos fills;
fa dos anys que no els ha enviat diners.
Un d'ells morirà d'aquí a uns instants
però jo no m'havia sentit mai
la meitat de viu de com em sent ara.

LECTOR

El primer vers és la porta que t'obre
la casa del poema. El que convida
a entrar i a posar-t'hi còmode.
La primera estrofa és la que et dóna
la benvinguda i t'arrossega a dins,
agafant-te pel braç i arrufant-se contra·tu;
la que et parla de calor i confiança
alhora que et fa seure a la butaca de la segona estrofa.

On has d'esperar que el sentit del poema
et porti un cafè, calent i dolç, per dar-te
alguna cosa perquè tinguis les mans
ocupades i no puguis desviar l'atenció
o agafar un diari del revister.

Ben aviat entrarà la conclusió
per la porta del darrere,
silenciosament i de puntes,
mentre el volum de la música augmenta
i és quan, per fi, intueixes que tothom
ja sap si la mà que amaga a l'esquena
porta una carta d'amor
o un punyal.

It's only three days they've ridden together.
Now it's months since they took a bath.
For three days they have been waiting
for the moment of the explosion that will free
a bullet from its bronze hiding-place.

One of them wears round his neck an Indian charm
(how he happens to have it is another story).
One of them has never shot a man in the back.
One of them has never felt so alive as he is now.

One of them left behind a wife and two children;
it's two years since he sent them any money.
One of them will die in just a few moments
but I have never felt
half as alive as I feel now.

READER

The first line is the door that opens for you
the house of the poem. The one that invites you
to come in and make yourself comfortable.
The first stanza is the one that welcomes
you and drags you inside,
grabbing you by the arm and frowning at you;
the one that speaks to you with warmth and trust
while it makes you sit down in the armchair of the second stanza.

Where you have to wait for the meaning of the poem
to bring you a coffee, hot and sweet, to give you
something so as to make sure your hands
are occupied and you don't lose concentration
or pick up a newspaper from the rack.

Soon the conclusion will arrive
through the back door,
silently and on tiptoe,
while the volume of the music rises
and it is when, at last, you intuit that everyone
already knows whether the hand hidden behind his back
holds a love-letter
or a dagger.

EL CONTRACTE

A cada cop el clau s'enfonsa més
en la peülla i el ferrador en corregeix
la inclinació amb martellades laterals.

A cada cop de l'home contra l'unglot
el cavall s'estremeix.

Només el costum el fa restar immòbil.
És el costum. La seva sang no recorda
haver estat un poltre entre iurtes mongols;
haver flanquejat les falanges d'Alexandre;
les càrregues en què ha mossegat i pegat coces.

La seva pell no recorda el llim del Nil
ni les arenes d'Aràbia,
no pot recordar els carretons i les caravanes,
ni la visió d'un ramat d'egües vora un llac.

Ell no sap res del so de les petjades
dels soldats darrere seu. Als cascs
no ha conegut el terra de granit
d'un Arc de Triomf i no l'ha escalfat
el marbre calent d'Hagia Sophia en flames.

Els cops rítmics del martell del ferrador
no li serveixen per fer memòria
del colpejar contra el flanc de la motxilla
del pony express, la seva boca no recorda
les llagues de l'embocadura, els esperons als flancs;
ni la suor recompensada pel triomf
ni les fuetades que són filles de les curses perdudes.

Cada ferradura és un contracte en semicercle
que renovam periòdicament i que diu:
a cops t'estimo, sempre et necessito,
porta't bé; potser fruiràs la misericòrdia
d'una bala i potser, quan siguis vell,
fins i tot esdevindràs carn.

THE CONTRACT

With each blow the nail is driven deeper
into the hoof and the blacksmith corrects
the angle with sideways blows of the hammer.

With each blow the man makes against the hoof
the horse shudders.

Only habit makes it keep still.
It is habit. Its blood holds no memory
of having been a foal among mongol yurts;
of having flanked the phalanxes of Alexander;
the loads under which it bit and kicked.

Its hide does not remember the mud of the Nile
or the sands of Arabia,
it cannot remember the carts and caravans,
nor the vision of a herd of mares beside a lake.

It knows nothing of the sound of tramping
soldiers behind it. Under its hooves
it has not known the granite rock
of a Triumphal Arch and has not been scorched
by the hot marble of Hagia Sofia in flames.

The blacksmith's rhythmic hammer-blows
in no way help it to remember
the way the saddlebag of the pony-express
would bang against its flank, its mouth does not recall
the sores the bit made, the spurs in its flanks;
nor its sweat rewarded by victory
or the whippings that are the offspring of races lost.

Every horseshoe is a semicircular contract
that we renew regularly and which says:
with blows we love you, we always have need of you,
behave well; perhaps you will be granted the mercy
of a bullet and maybe, when you are old,
you will even become meat.

ELIES BARBERÀ

PHOTO: MARINA COLLADO BENNASAR

ELIES BARBERÀ (born Xàtiva, 1970) is an actor and a poet. His written works include *Quaranta contes breus i un llarguíssim poema d'amor* (Forty Short Stories and a Long Love Poem, 2000), and the poetry collections, *Mata-rates (i altres vicis)* (Rotgut (and other vices), 2003), *Equilibrista* (2004), *Zoo* (2007), *Aixàtiva, Aixàtiva* (Ah, Xàtiva, Xàtiva, 2008) and *Allà on les grues nien* (Where the Cranes Nest, 2009). His most recent publication is entitled *En la Primavera perpètua* (In Perpetual Spring, 2010), a play made up of poetic texts.

In 2008 he participated in the 'Parallel Voices' exchange program, as a result of which the Institute of Catalan Literature published the anthology *De l'Atles a Formentor* (From the Atlas Mountains to Formentor), and in 2011 he participated in the twentieth Seminar in Poetic Translation, held in Farrera de Pallars and Marseilles, also organized by the Institute of Catalan Literature.

Other collaborations towards which he has contributed include: *100 són 100* (100 is 100, 2007), *For Sale o 50 veus de la terra* (For Sale or 50 Voices of the Earth, 2010), and the anthology *Tibar l'arc* (Drawing the Bow, 2012) published by Tria Llibres.

DISSORTAT MICKEY MOUSE

«Pobre Mickey Mouse»
                              mussiten veus borratxes de sirenes.
Pobre Mickey Mouse,
l'aspecte fred de Minnie t'ha sobtat.
No t'ho podies cavil·lar,
però els seus mots tallaven com ganivets o ullals.
I avui t'ha dit que no
                    que prou
                    que mai més, Mickey Mouse.
I tot s'ha ensorrat:
la plàstica felicitat americana s'ha ensorrat,
l'efímera felicitat burgesa.
I una fogonada t'ha crescut consciència endins:
l'angoixa,
            el marejol…

«Pobre Mickey Mouse»,
                              mussiten veus borratxes de sirenes.
Camines, Mickey Mouse,
per avingudes buides com la nit,
humides pobrament
d'aquesta gasa d'aigua com un plor,
tacades de neons obscens.

Passeges, Mickey Mouse, fantasma amb gavardina.
les sabates roges esclafeixen com assots al terra brut.
La nit és una rata de mil rostres
i tu ets ara una rata trista.
I rates-dones mouen cues, mouen llavis, mouen culs
i et pregunten ¿quines coses, rata trista?
Però buscaràs abans un bar on ofegar el teu honor,
el teu honor… i el teu bon nom: Mickey Mouse, de Disney.
I al cap dels whiskys màgics n'eixiràs
i respondràs a la veu de rata-dona de neó que et diga ¿quines
                                          coses, rata trista?
I junts marxareu bulevard avall
i no voldràs saber el llit en què t'aixecaràs demà.

UNLUCKY MICKEY MOUSE

"Poor Mickey Mouse"
                    drunken siren voices mumble.
Poor Mickey Mouse,
Minnie's icy glance has caught you on the back foot.
You couldn't dwell on it,
but her words cut you like knives or fangs.
And today she just said no to you
                    that that's enough
                    …and, no more, Mickey Mouse.
And everything has collapsed around you:
the plastic American happiness has collapsed,
that ephemeral bourgeois happiness.
And an explosion has gone on growing deep in your consciousness:
anguish,
          and nausea…

"Poor Mickey Mouse!"
                    drunken siren voices mumble.
Mickey Mouse, you are walking
down avenues as empty as the night,
feebly dampened
by this gauze of water like a fit of weeping,
and soiled by obscene neon signs.

Mickey Mouse, you are strolling, a ghost dressed in a raincoat,
your red shoes cracking out like whips on filthy ground.
Night is a mouse with a thousand faces
and you are now a sad mouse.
And lady-mice move their tails, move their lips, move their bums
and ask you What's the matter, sad mouse?
But first you'll find a bar where you can drown your honour,
your honour… and your good name: Mickey Mouse, from Disney.
And after those magic whiskeys you'll go out
and you'll answer the voice of a neon lady-mouse that calls, What's
                                        the matter, sad mouse?
And you'll walk together down the boulevard
and you won't want to know what bed you'll wake up in tomorrow.

AUTUMN LEAVES

«Podria fer-ho amb una noia
menuda, com de marfil»
GABRIEL FERRATER

Avui podria enamorar-me de qualsevol dameta de cames cristal·lines,
llargues cames de cristall com dos versos de Saint-John Perse
avui podria
avui podria sortir a passejar
ara que és de nit, discretament,
les mans dins dels pulmons calents i violacis,
sortir a passejar
ara que és tardor
posat d'abric com un gat sense sostre
i buscar un cau acollidor, de tèbia llum i bona música – Stan Getz,
                                        posem per cas –
i asseure'm al taulell, com un heroi caduc, groguenc, de les
novel·les policíaques demanar una cervesa qualsevol – per
dissimular – clissar la clientela femenina
o millor,
clissar les cames fines de la digna clientela femenina,
arrecerades sota taules circulars de marbre sec les cames
demanar dos gintònics successius, pacients gintònics del valor,
i amb calma extàtica, com un deliri mesurat, beure'ls sense febre
i triar, amb temps i pols, la propietària de llargues cames fines
                                        de cristall
i esperar l'instant felí per encetar somriures com roselles

sí, avui podria
avui podria
podria
podria...

m'agrada el mode viatger, condicional dels verbs

HIMNE DELS COVARDS

va nàixer l'any 70
el cel era un desert metàl·lic sense núvols
sobre la pell de pergamí del cadàver del país on va nàixer
no volaven els ocells ni els poetes
sobre el crani de vaca del cadàver del país on va nàixer

AUTUMN LEAVES

> "I could do it with a tiny
> girl, maybe made of ivory"
> GABRIEL FERRATER

Today I could fall in love with any little lady with crystalline legs,
long legs made of glass like two lines by Saint-John Perse
today I could
today I could go for a walk
now that it is night, discreetly,
hands inside my hot, purplish lungs,
go for a walk
now that it is autumn
with my warm coat on like a cat on the tiles
and look for a welcoming den, with warm light and good music –
                                        Stan Getz, for example –
and sit at the bar, like an old, sallow-faced hero from a
detective story and ask for any old beer – to
pretend – and scan the feminine clientele
or rather,
scan the slender legs of the excellent feminine clientele,
legs below round tables whose dry marble tops conceal them
ask for two gin-and-tonics on the trot, patient, brave gin-and-tonics,
and with ecstatic calm, like a measured delirium, drink them quietly
and choose, steadily, taking my time, the owner of long, slender
                                        legs made of glass
and await the happy moment for smiles to open like poppies

yes, today I could
today I could,
I could
I could…

I like the travelling, conditional mode of the verb

THE COWARD'S HYMN

he was born in 1970
the sky was a metallic desert with no clouds
on the parchment skin of the corpse of the country where he was born
no birds were flying and no poets
over the cow's skull of the corpse of the country where he was born

no corrien ja felins ni savis
degotaven les aixetes i la queda era de plom
no florien roses de les conques d'ulls de calaveres espantades
soterrades per la pala de la guerra
ni roselles ni fenolls
només el tuf d'Oblit omplia com l'àcid
sales blaves d'hospital fantasmagòric
hi havia un malalt i tothom ho sabia
hi havia un malalt gegant gitat jagut
sobre gorres de nens
i sobre els caps dels pares silenciats
uns homes de bigoti
servien al malalt culleretes d'aigua amb sucre
i el malalt no es deixava tocar per bales d'Odi

en aquest desert de mans va créixer com tants d'altres creixien:
sense terra sota els peus
perquè els l'havien negada del petroli del no-res
sense records dels grans
perquè deien que el gat immens de la postguerra
els havia menjat la llengua de la Memòria
sí va créixer com tants d'altres: sense lligams
sense abraçades
sense consciència els feien a les escoles d'uniforme
de mitjons blancs els regles la creu encara plovia moria aquell home
sense consciència
els feien
però com la febre la Consciència arribava un dia qualsevol
mentre un es botonava la camisa davant l'espill
i s'atrevia a mirar-se el pit
la basarda no calia ensenyar-la a escola
l'havien mamada dels mugrons de les mares
i els corria per dins com un element més de la sang
els adoctrinaren en covardia en dogmes inútils
en l'art tan noble del silenci i de l'oblit
sense dolor a les genives de l'ànima

i així ha pujat aquesta generació frontissa
entre vells costums de mans pansides de rectors sobre negre de sotana
i nous costums capitalistes de plàstics i encenalls: *it's o.k.*
ha après a viure a 160 km/h exigències del mercat
a quant el cafís de dòlars? a canvi de què?
el pinyol de l'angoixa i l'espina de la infelicitat
entravessats a la gola seua de cada dia

now no felines ran nor wise men
the taps dripped and the curfew bell was made of lead
no roses flowered in the eye sockets of terrified skulls
buried by the shovel of war
neither poppies nor fennel
only the stink of oblivion filled like acid
the blue wards of a ghostly hospital
there was a sick giant and everyone knew it
there was a giant lying bedded
on children's bonnets
and on the heads of the silenced parents
men with moustaches
fed the sick man spoonfuls of sugared water
and the sick man did not let himself be shot by the bullets of hatred

in this desert of hands he grew up as so many others grew up:
with no land beneath his feet
because they had drowned it in the petroleum of nothingness
with no memory on the part of the grown-ups
because they said that the huge postwar cat
had eaten Memory's tongue
yes he grew up like so many others: without ties
without caresses
without conscience they made them uniform in schools
in white socks the rules the cross still rained that man was dying
without conscience
they made them
but like fever Conscience was coming one of those days
while he was buttoning his shirt in front of the mirror
and he dared to look at his breast
fear was something you weren't to show at school
it had been suckled by the teats of mothers
and flowed inside them like one more element in the blood
they indoctrinated them in cowardice in useless dogmas
in the noble art of silence and oblivion
painless to the gums of the soul

and thus this interface generation has climbed
between old customs of withered hands of priests on black soutanes
and new capitalist customs of plastics and passing phases: *it's o.k.*
he has learned to live at 160 kmph market imperatives
what is a bushel of dollars worth? in exchange for what?
the stone of anguish and the thorn of misery
caught every day in his throat

ORATORI

oh Gran Mare Llar Gran Casa Ciutat
ossam de mamut ventre de balena
gegant escapçat altar de petroli
sala de motors submarí en vigília
urna de grisú estómac de rata
úter enquistat quasi cancerós
escolta els teus fills Única Metròpoli
i com fas ara segueix protegint-los
del monstre voraç que ells mateixos són
i guarda'ls de l'espúria ombra del tu
empara'ls de mirades com revòlvers
salva'ls de l'olor i la veu de l'altre
de la mà estranya i la carnalitat
la proximitat la perplexitat
salva'ls del combat fes saltar els ponts
tal com ara ho fas no demanen més
preserva'ls Mare de l'infern dels altres
vetla pels teus fills humils Gran Ciutat
i proporciona'ls tots els mitjans
d'aïllament forçós més escaients:
que el fulgor tan blanc de la netedat
l'asèpsia de l'anorreament
i la incurable fenella entre els homes
seguesquen per sempre vivint amb ells
i els facen persistir en solitud
al bosc dels arbres alts i els rostres erms
són cadells humans porucs què hi farem?
protegeix-los Mare embolcalla'ls Llar
Gran Casa Ciutat Única Metròpoli
formiguer formidable entre deserts
virus de ciment que creixes per sobre
les fites i fronteres dels antics
Gran Mare Ciutat a tu s'encomanen!

lluny dels suburbis metropolitans
potser els bàrbars fan les seues guerres
o pacten treves amb tribus del nord
o abillats els turmells de cascavells
potser celebren festes en honor
als vells déus estrangers i estrafolaris

ORATORY

oh, Great Hearth Mother Great Home City
mammoth bones whale belly
beheaded giant altar to petroleum
engine-room watchful submarine
urn full of firedamp rat's stomach
encysted, almost cancerous womb
hear your sons Unique Metropolis
and as you do now go on protecting them
from the voracious monster that they are
and keep them from the spurious shadow of yourself
protect them from glances like revolvers
save them from the smell and voice of the other
from the hand of a stranger and from carnality
proximity and perplexity
rescue them from war blow the bridges up
the way you do now they ask nothing more
preserve the Mother from others' hell
watch over your humble children Great City
and award them all the most suitable
means of compulsory isolation:
may the dazzling white of cleanliness
the asepsis of annihilation
and the incurable split between men
all continue to dwell with them
and make them persist in their solitude
in the forest of tall trees and wild faces
they are fearful human pups what can we do with them?
Protect them Mother swaddle them Hearth
Great Home City Unique Metropolis
formidable anthill among deserts
cement virus growing on top of
the boundaries and frontiers of the ancients
Great Mother City to you they commend themselves!

far from the city suburbs
maybe the barbarians wage their wars
or agree truces with northern tribes
or with ankles adorned with bells
maybe they celebrate festivals
in honour of old, foreign and outlandish gods

CENDRES A LES CENDRES

arriben nous ídols. els flaixos de les càmeres. els aeroports. hem
instal·lat els nous ídols sobre peanyes de plàstic. la funcionalitat,
ja se sap. Jesucrist amb el 10 a l'esquena i rampes a les cames
intenta la darrera incursió per la banda. mor el cristianisme a
occident. minva la flama. lentament. una preclara agonia. salta
l'alarma. els titulars de la premsa esportiva. hom encén espel-
mes de colors als peus dels nous ídols. hosanna! en solem tenir
notícia per televisió. abatut, vaporós com un fantasma, Jesucrist
abandona el camp de joc. s'apaguen els llums de l'estadi. el des-
crèdit. la vella samarreta xopa de suor, feta un manyoc, al terra
del vestuari. exsangüe retorna al sepulcre d'on fa 20 segles havia
ressuscitat. cristal·litza per fi cadàver. cendres a les cendres. ben
mirat el cristianisme s'havia bastit sobre el cadàver de l'ídol.

OLOR PRIMERA

l'olor primera que recorde
és la que amarava el casal
on s'encabia la segona
escola de pàrvuls, al cap
del carrer doctor Blasco Soto:
olor a Terra, i humitat
que n'emergeix, vapor que em mulla,
terra dels camps, simplicitat
indestriable, alé, saó,
bàlsam de Terra ungint les mans.

i quan passege per allà
escrute a una banda i a l'altra
del carrer; si ningú no em veu
si no hi vagareja ni una ànima,
amb recel de dragó d'estiu
m'arrape al portaló de fusta;
ver i voraç saquejador
l'animaló que presa ensuma:
d'aquella olor
no queda res:
flaire el Record
– vibrant i espés –
narius endins

ASHES TO ASHES

new idols arrive, cameras flash, airports, we have erected the new idols on pedestals made of plastic, their usefulness, we know all about that. Jesus Christ with the 10 on the left and cramp in his legs attempts the final incursion on the side. christianity dies in the west. the flame dwindles. slowly. an illustrious agony. the alarm goes off. officials of the sporting press. a man lights coloured candles at the feet of new idols. hosanna! we generally hear news of this on television. beaten, cloudy as a ghost, Jesus Christ leaves the field of play. the lights in the stadium go out. disrepute. the old T-shirt wet with sweat, nothing but a bundle on the dressing-room floor. he goes, bloodless, back to the tomb from which 20 centuries ago he had risen. a corpse at last he crystallizes. ashes to ashes. when you look at it christianity had been built upon the corpse of the idol.

EARLIEST SMELL

the earliest smell I remember
is the one that pervaded the old manor
where the second infant school
was housed, at the top
of Dr Blasco Soto street:
the smell of Earth, and humidity
that rises from it, vapour that drenches me,
earth of the fields, ineffable
simplicity, breath, ripeness,
balsam of Earth anointing my hands.

and when I walk that way
I look carefully to one side of the street
and the other; if no one sees me
if there's not a soul wandering about,
with the wariness of a summer gecko
I grip the wooden porch;
true and voracious plunderer
the tiny beast that, when captured, scents it:
of that smell
nothing remains:
Memory sniffs –
thick and vibrant –
nostrils deep inside

de la Memòria:
simplicitat
de terra molla
pedram humit.
ja tinc quatre anys.

20 N 75, DIA DE BASSES

feia dies que aquella pluja
durava: els últims 40 anys,
per ser més exactes, i el pati
de l'escola esdevingué un llac.
ens torbava una tardor tèrbola,
com la caputxa de les bruixes;
l'aigua més amunt dels turmells,
estalvis dins les catiüsques.
fent d'ham la pica del paraigua
pescàvem un llombrígol ert
botinflat com una variu
copat per l'aigua del Leteu…
sobtadament, com mai, sonaren
els timbals de la inquietud,
les sirenes; formàrem files
i ens botiren dins l'autobús.
i als carrers, vaticinis, veus…
les boques de tots els megàfons
– gesmils florint als millors temps –
proclamaven la mort d'en Franco.

MARAGDES

llobera endins penetra i ara el Xino
ja no és mai més raval, sinó rovell,
sinó epicentre, eclosió de vida:
pels carrerons corren les veus, les pells
de tot el món. i com l'heura s'enfila
per balcons i façanes la Babel
possible, lava imparable del viure.
sent la cançó del mall i dels martells,
de les esquenes, dels braons que aixequen
els murs, dels peus somorts i molls d'obrers.

what is Remembered:
simplicity
of moist earth
damps stones.
I am four years old once more.

20 NOV 75, DAY OF PONDS

for days now the rain had gone on
falling: for the last 40 years,
to be more precise, and the playground
at school became a lake.
a cloudy autumn pressed down on us,
like the pointed hat worn by witches;
water above our ankles –
safe inside our welly boots.
using an umbrella spike as a hook
we fished up a stiff earthworm
swollen like a varicose vein
hit by the water of Lethe…
suddenly, as never before, drums
of disquiet rang out,
the sirens; we lined up
and they stuffed us into a bus,
and in the streets, prophesies, voices…
everyone's mouths megaphones –
jasmine flowering in better times –
proclaiming the death of Franco.

EMERALDS

deeper into the lair he goes and now the *barri Xino*
is no longer outskirts, or shell, but rather yolk,
or rather epicentre, explosion of life:
along the alleys run the voices, the skins
of the whole world, and like ivy creeping
over balconies and façades the possible
Babel, the unstoppable lava of living.
he hears the song of the sledge-hammer, joiners' hammers,
song of the bent backs, of the arms that raise up
walls, of the soft and muffled feet of workers.

pels carrerons, com bava de llimac
la humitat brilla en la pedra molsuda,
reumàtica maragda de la ionqui,
únic present per la polpa espremuda
de Lupita, la vella cupletista
que beu absenta a xarrup de cullera,
del proxeneta jove, del gitano,
del mariner marica amb gonorrea,
del nen nord-africà, de l'ancià,
de Margot, paquidèrmica estanquera,
dels predadors sedentaris, forçats
al tamboret del bar com corbs marins.
hi ha els carrerons plens i el tràfec i el comerç
i gats, coloms, hostals, terrats, matins,
gavines sobre la bugada estesa:
de ressaca de mar, l'aire florit.
disciplinadament a les voreres,
putes de tots sabors guarden la fila,
flors al femer caigut de Sant Ramon,
la bellesa i el riure entre enderrocs.
i una patrulla d'urbans avançant:
càmera lenta, botes altes, cascs,
plomalls, quadrigues llampants per les vies
de Roma: herois i roses i trompetes...
la reina de les meuques, desdentada
corona, mostra des del balancí
la desbarbada flor del frau marcit.
mes, qui entrarà a la casa esportellada?

pels carrerons, entre orins i llambordes,
corre la veu del Xino, l'elegia:
«Pigalle, t'invoque a tu, esperit canalla,
germà bessó de sang, d'arrel de vida!
I véns volant, ventíjol, llengua, flama,
i beses els braons suats dels nois
i vas grimpant per les parets leproses
i en les noies encens fanals i cors
i ets en el nen, la dona, l'home i l'avi,
Pigalle, Pigalle, oh, tu, esperit dels barris!».

Xino, solatge, maragda a la sang,
núvol ratat al fons de les mirades;
Xino, graella, laberint, cristalls,
rovell humit, alcova, cor i entranyes.

along the alleys, like a slug's trail
damp shines on mossy stone,
rheumatic emerald of the drug-addict,
only gift for the squeezed pulp
of Lupita, the old music-hall singer
who sips absinthe from a spoon,
of the young pimp, of the gypsy,
of the gay sailor with gonorrhea,
of the North African child, of the old, old man,
of Margot, leather-skinned tobacconist,
of the sedentary predators, old lags
like cormorants on stools at the bar.
there are the busy alleys and bustle and trade
and cats, pigeons, hostels, flat roofs, mornings,
gulls on the line with the washing:
the sea with its undertow, blossom in the air.
in orderly fashion along the pavements
whores of every flavour line up,
flowers on Sant Ramon's fallen dungheap,
beauty and laughter amongst the rubbish.
and a police patrol advancing:
slow-motion camera, jack-boots, helmets,
crests, chariots flashing along the roads
of Rome: heroes and roses and trumpets...
the queen of tarts, toothless
crown, displays from her rocking-chair
the shaved flower of withered fraud.
but, who will enter that breached house?

along the alleys, over urine and flagstones,
runs the *barri Xino's* voice, the elegy:
"Pigalle, you spirit of the streets,
my twin, blood-brother, sibling root of life!
And you come flying, breeze, tongue, flame,
and you kiss the sweating arms of boys
and you go climbing the leprous walls
and in girls you kindle lamps and hearts
and are in the child, the woman, man and grandfather,
Pigalle, Pigalle, you spirit of the streets!"

Xino, dregs, emerald in the blood,
threadbare cloud in the depths of glances;
Xino, window-bars, labyrinth, crystals,
damp rust, bedroom, heart and guts.

ARQUEÒLEG

s'obri el container forçant un badall
de desgana: grinyolen dins els molls.
la bafarada, el riure dels detritus.
mig engolit per la bocassa, l'home
del ganxo furga i remena en la brossa,
i un núvol de rantelles el saluda.
no defalleix. somnia en diamants,
tresors ocults en les escorrialles.
i troba en la negror del mut sarcòfag
una nina òrfena, parpella torta,
bonica com un pastisset, que el mira
poruga, i ell la cull d'aquell bressol
infecte i la carrega al carretó
d'articles de sagrada procedència
amb dolça i cerimoniosa cura.

GERMANA ANORÈXIA

Sobre potetes d'au va l'Anorèxia
i duu en la sang la fosca voluntat
de dissipació: desaparéixer,
fulgir en l'abandó, l'estel fugaç.
I així, a la minva, prear-se, estimar-se.
Fulgir, desaparéixer com els àngels,
com llum, com vol de fada, com el pol·len
davant els ulls atònits de la Vaca
– el tòtem vigorós de l'abundància –
que es meravella i mai no ho comprendrà.
«Però digues, estimada, els teus noms.»
«Els meus noms són:
canell, genoll,
estern, clavícula,
ròtula, fèmur,
vèrtebra, tíbia,
húmer, calcani,
còccix i cúbit,
maxil·lar, pòmul,
isqui, ili i radi.»
«Així, llebrer bidimensional,
així et lluu l'os emergint a besllums

ARCHAEOLOGIST

he has the container opened forcing a reluctant
gap: a screeching in the machinery.
the reek, the laughter of garbage.
half-smothered by the fetid breath, the man
with the hook pokes and prods among the rubbish,
and a cloud of mosquitoes greets him.
he doesn't weaken, he dreams of diamonds,
treasures hidden among the refuse.
and finds in the blackness of the mute sarcophagus
an orphan girl-child, one eyelid askew,
as pretty as a little cake, who looks at him
fearfully, and he plucks her from that foul
cradle and carries her over to the trailer
that waits for articles of sacred origin
with gentle and ceremonious care.

SISTER ANOREXIA

Anorexia walks on little bird-like legs
and carries in her blood the dark desire
for destruction: to disappear,
to shine in renunciation, the shooting star.
And thus, by shrinking, to value oneself, love oneself.
To shine, to vanish like angels,
like light, like the flight of a fairy, like pollen
before the astonished eyes of the Cow –
the vigorous emblem of abundance –
who marvels and will never understand it.
"But tell me, dearest, your names."
"My names are:
wrist, knee,
breast-bone, collar-bone,
patella, femur,
vertebra, tibia,
humerus, heel-bone
coccyx and elbow,
jawbone, cheekbone,
hip-bone, ileus and radius."
"And so, two-dimensional greyhound,
and so your bone shines, shines through, emerging

així, cap d'iceberg, entranya gèlida
així, blancor groguenca i bonyeguda.
Fins fer-se seda s'estova la pell.
Del teu somriure esquerdat, calavera,
alguna fibra es trenca en la ganyota.
Reina de nucs i articulacions.
Acordió de carn malmesa. Esput.
La lenta eruga de la malaltia
articulada sobre l'encisam
regira els seus segments ressecs i verds.
Flauta lilosa del fos esquelet,
lied per a violí, passada d'arc
sobre les cordes, cadència, llàgrima;
fagot llarguíssim filtra l'alegria
i la victòria de vint grams menys:
plores felicitat a la balança:
el pes que no. Desaparició.
Perquè així et mostres:
insectívora, agònica
pregramítica, afònica
tarantúlica, aràcnida
barbitúrica, tàntrica
pergamínica, tètrica
serafínica, mètrica
dramàtica, plutònica
antàrtica, octopòdica
maniàtica
programàtica
postromàntica
quiromàntica
calavèrica
catalèptica
iogurtèrica
epilèptica
cadavèrica
malencònica
espasmòdica
halitòsica
fractalfílica
policlínica
paroxística,
així te'm mostres,
aranya blanca d'escàs moviment
que teixeixes la tova teranyina
on seràs tu mateixa perla i mort».

and so, tip of an iceberg, frozen gut
and so, yellowish, bumpy whiteness.
The skin softens until it turns to silk.
Some thread snaps in the grimace
of your twisted smile, skull.
Queen of knuckles and joints.
Accordion of ill-dressed flesh. Spittle.
The slow caterpillar of sickness
hooped over the lettuce
twists and turns its green and skinny segments.
Lilac-coloured flute of the wasted skeleton,
lied for violin, bow-stroke
over the strings, cadence, tear;
extra-long bassoon filtering the joy
and the victory of a twenty-gram loss:
you weep happiness on the scales:
the no-weight. Disappearance.
Because this is how you show yourself:
insectivorous, agonic
pre-gram-manic, aphonic
tarantulic, arachnid
barbituric, tantric
parchmenteric, tetric
seraphysic, metric
dramatic, plutonic
antarctic, octopedic
manic
programmatic
postromantic
chiromantic
craniologic
cataleptic
yoghurteric
epileptic
abracadaveric
melancholic
spasmodic
halitosic
fractalphilic
polyclinic
paroxystic,
so you show yourself to me,
white spider of scant movement
weaving your soft web
where you yourself will be both pearl and death."

POLÍGON

són les vuit de la nit dins l'autobús.
humana o animal hi ha una fortor,
un tall podrit de cansalada espessa
que el ganivet del nas fendeix en dos.
i a fora, pels carrers esgrogueïts
camegen les persones a tentines
sense cançons, ni balls, ni temps, ni anhels,
collat l'alé, callat l'humor i el riure.
la sageta roent del desencant
esgarra el cel de les biografies:
del que hom volia ser al que ara s'és!
retrats ratats, parracs de rastre i vidre.

semàfors i semàfors i semàfors…
vehicles i vehicles i vehicles…
creix la Ciutat com una taca d'oli
i allà també les grues grogues nien.
la xarxa extensa esdevenint polígon,
geometria, massa industrial,
llei progressiva de mutació.
pas de frontera, paratges d'asfalt,
ribes d'acer i crestes d'uralita.
ací les rates acacen als gats.
esbalaïdes canten les sirenes:
canvi de torn, bull el polígon ara.
canvi d'obrers, els llums de fre dels cotxes
són cuques roges, processionària.
momificar-se cada dia més
en la melassa amorfa que asfixia.
submergir, deixatar la Consciència,
amnèsia àcida de l'aigua alisa.
perquè hi ha podridures sense olor
camí de pètals, jornal de deu hores,
catifes roges dels treballadors.
amb cotxes es desplacen fins la fàbrica
– mateixa escuderia que els de l'amo.
si això era la Igualtat, avant i hosanna! –
i entren als esportius: vidres fumats,
la clau, brum-brum, l'ària del motor,
frec de vellut a l'accelerador
– mateix frec de vellut que l'amo sent.
amén, doncs, si era això la Llibertat! –

INDUSTRIAL ESTATE

it's eight o'clock in the evening in the bus.
human or animal there is a stink,
a rotten slice of thick pork fat
that the blade of the nose cuts in two.
and outside, along the yellowish streets
people stumble and grope their way
with no songs, no dancing, no time, no longings,
breath collared, humour and laughter stifled.
the white-hot arrow of disenchantment
despoils the sky of human lives:
of what man wanted to be and what he now is!
gnawed portraits, trailing rags and glass.

traffic-lights and traffic-lights and traffic-lights…
vehicles and vehicles and vehicles…
the City is spreading like a pool of oil
and there too the yellow cranes nest.
the spreading net becoming industrial estate,
geometry, industrial mass,
progressive law of mutation.
no frontier, asphalt places,
steel banks and ridges of uralite.
here the rats hunt the cats.
in terror the sirens wail:
change of shift, the industrial estate's now buzzing.
workers change over, brake-lights on cars
are red caterpillars, processionaries.
mummifying yourself more each day
asphyxiated in amorphous treacle.
go under, let your conscience grow weak,
acid amnesia of tasteless water.
because there are rotting things that have no smell
petalled path, ten-hour day,
red carpets for the workers.
they drive in cars to the factory –
same livery as the boss's.
if that means Equality, onward and excelsior! –
and they get into their sports cars: smoked glass,
ignition, brum-brum, the engine's aria,
velvet friction on the accelerator –
the same velvet friction the boss feels.
amen, then, if that was Liberty! –

i en la nit fugen, fantasmes discrets.
altres senyals i divises ignoren
perquè només l'obrer s'embruta al toll,
perquè només per ell sona el xiulet
de les hores, dels còmputs, de les portes,
i només a l'obrer el jou estreny.
l'eficiència, una obsessió.
exigències rases del Sistema.
les peces dins de l'Ordre imperatiu!
«Fanfàrries de l'èxit ens saluden,
triomfals sota el pal·li del progrés
avancem, sí!…
            Cap a quin paradís?
Quantes medalles d'or mereixerem?».

les deu. la nit. la plana industrial.
d'alguna nau arriben llums i boires.
que no paren les dents dels engranatges!
que politges i torns i cintes roden!
la confiança en el castell de naips,
seguit-seguit prospera la cadena.
illes, fractures, terratrèmols, falles
esclaten lluny. preservem el Sistema.

and they speed away into the night, discreet ghosts.
other signals and emblems don't know
why only the worker gets dirty in the pool
because for him alone the whistle blows
the hours, the reckoning, the gates,
and the worker alone is crushed by the yoke.
efficiency, an obsession.
basic requirements of the System.
the pieces in an imperative Order!
"Fanfares at the exit salute us,
triumphant beneath the pallium of progress
let us advance, yes!...
        Towards what paradise?
How many gold medals shall we deserve?"

ten o'clock at night, the industrial zone.
the lights and fogs of some ship are approaching.
may the cogs of the gears go on holding!
may pulleys and winches and belts go on turning!
the trust in a house of cards,
the production-line prospers without ceasing.
islands, fractures, earthquakes, breakdowns
erupt far-off, let us preserve the System.

JORDI JULIÀ

PHOTO: AUTHOR'S ARCHIVE

JORDI JULIÀ (born Sant Celoni, 1972) is a poet, essayist and professor of Literary Theory and Comparative Literature at the Autonomous University of Barcelona. He specializes in the study of contemporary literature and his critical works have received both national and international awards. Some of the titles published in Catalan and Spanish include: *Al marge dels versos* (Besides the Verses, 1998), *Un segle de lectura* (A Century of Reading, 2001), *La perspectiva contemporánea* (Contemporary Perspective, 2004), *Modernitat del món fungible* (Modernity of the Replaceable World, 2006), *L'art imaginatiu* (The Imaginative Art, 2007), *Dietari de lectures* (Reading Diary, 2009), and *Poètica de l'exili* (Poetics of Exile, 2011).

Although his poetry has received many awards across the region of Catalonia, his work is still little known. Some of his recently published books of poetry include: *Hiverns suaus* (Mild Winters, 2005), *Sota la llum de Mart* (Under the Light of Mars, 2006), *Els déus de fang* (The Gods of Mud, 2007), *Principi de plaer* (The Pleasure Principle, 2007), *Planisferi lunar* (Lunar Planisphere, 2008), *Un lleu plugim* (A Gentle Rain, 2009), *Poètica per a un ninot* (Poetics for a Doll) and *Circumstàncies adverses* (Adverse Circumstances, both published in 2011), and *Gent forastera* (Foreign People, 2012).

MIRADES

Breaking home ties, 1954

Potser devia ser una estació petita,
allunyada del ranxo. No hi ha més passatgers
que s'esperin pel tren, i enmig de tots els camps
van cruixint les llagostes, com un turment etern.
La jove il·lusió es mostra als ulls atents d'un noi,
que allarga una mirada de resolta impaciència
cap a una llunyania que confon els rails
en un punt d'horitzó. Els ulls tristos d'un gos
miren amb lassitud cap a aquest mateix lloc,
no sap què fan aquí però intueix la pèrdua
i recolza el musell a sobre del genoll
del seu amo més jove, com sempre havia fet,
esperant una mà que ha anat creixent de mida
i comença a mancar-li: els dos palmells apreten
el paquet del dinar, lligat amb cinta rosa,
que li ha donat la mare abans de dir-li adéu
i anar-se fent petita, agitant la mà al porxo.
Al seu costat el pare, amb l'esquena vinclada
de tanta feina dura entre terra i bestiar;
entre les mans aguanta el seu barret i el nou
que li han comprat al fill, que estrena un vestit *beige*
i porta una corbata que van trobar a l'armari.
Els fondos ulls del pare miren cap a la terra
– que tant l'ha fet suar, que ha ressecat el sol,
que li ha cremat la pell – per on passa la via
que s'ha d'emportar el nen, ben lluny d'aquesta vida,
a una ciutat del nord amb professors i llibres.
Enganxada als seus llavis manté una cigarreta
encara per encendre, i entre els dits un llumí
preparat per gastar quan aparegui el tren
i a l'hora del comiat una abraçada ferma,
d'home a home, provoqui una mirada humida:
dirà, llavors, que el fum se li ha ficat als ulls.

CARAMEL

Passejo dins la boca dues lletres
repetides que formen el teu nom.
Salivo gust de mel, maduixa i sucre,

GLANCES

Breaking home ties, 1954

I guess it must have been a small station,
a long way from the ranch. There are no other passengers
waiting for the train, and in the middle of every field
the grasshoppers go on crunching, like an endless torment.
Youthful excitement shines in the alert eyes of a boy,
who lets a glance of resolute impatience stretch out
into the far-off distance that melts the rails
at a point on the horizon. The sad eyes of a dog
gaze wearily towards this same place,
not knowing what is afoot but intuiting loss
and he leans his muzzle on the knee
of his younger master, as he has always done,
waiting for a hand that has gone on growing in size
and which he begins to miss: both palms grip
the lunch parcel, tied with pink ribbon,
which his mother gave him before saying goodbye
and dwindling, waving her hand from the porch.
Beside him his father, with back bent
from so much hard toil between soil and cattle;
holding tightly in his hands his hat and the new one
bought for the boy, who wears for the first time a beige suit
and a tie they dug out of the wardrobe.
The father's deep eyes gaze downwards at the soil –
that has made him sweat and sweat, that the sun has baked,
that has burned his skin – where the tracks lie
which are to carry the boy away, far away from this life,
to a northern city with teachers and books.
Stuck to his lip, a cigarette dangles,
yet to be lit, and between his fingers a match
ready to be struck when the train appears
and, at the moment of farewell, a firm hug,
man to man, that may cause his eyes to moisten:
he will say, then, that the smoke got in his eyes.

TOFFEE

I promenade around my mouth the two letters
which, repeated, make up your name.
My saliva tastes of honey, strawberry and sugar,

i el passo per les galtes, per la llengua,
i el faig jugar amb les dents més esmolades
a que hi xoqui i es deixi mossegar.
De tant en tant s'enganxa al paladar,
o em crema les genives, fins que es llima;
llavors es torna un peix – sabó dins l'aigua –,
s'escapa, se m'amaga i deixa aroma
de llor quan, com un déu, torno a encalçar-lo.
Però de tant jugar a cuita-amagar,
després d'assaborir-lo sense fre,
se m'ha anat fent petit, se m'ha aprimat,
s'ha esmolat com la fulla de l'acer,
i ha fet sagnar-me els llavis que el van prendre,
van aprendre'l, i no el podran no dir.

ELS DISSABTES DELS HOMES

Aposten el que tenen al vermell
d'una nit de dissabte que els permeti
una vida millor que faci oblit
de tantes feines que preferirien
no haver de fer al cap d'un dia llarg,
que puguin venerar els caps de setmana
per poder creure que la realitat
no es troba al mig de dilluns i divendres.
Dissabte es lleven tard i compraran
per tota la setmana, i queden junts
per poder anar a sopar, i a bars de nit
per parlar de les coses que els importen:
els cotxes, el futbol, diners i dones.
I acaben tots dins d'entresols fosquíssims
plens de llums, i de fum, i de xivarri.
Fumen i beuen molt, i parlen alt
a prop d'unes orelles que no volen
escoltar-los. I fan veure que ballen,
fins que es cansen i tornen a assetjar
algú que sembla fer-los molt més cas,
afalagada amb les plasenteries
que hauran sabut mentir – no prou
com perquè els acompanyi fins al llit.
I tornen a fumar i a beure, i mouen
un cos que està cansat de tanta nit.

and I pass it from cheek to cheek, over my tongue,
and make it play with my sharpest teeth
so that it clings and lets itself be bitten.
Now and then it sticks to my palate,
or burns my gums, until it's really smooth;
then it turns into a fish – a piece of soap in water –
escapes, hides from me and leaves a
taste of laurel when, like a god, I go back and hunt it down.
But from playing so long at hide-and-seek,
after relishing it wantonly,
it has gone all small and thin on me,
gone sharp like a razor-blade,
and has made bleed the lips that ate it,
they learned it, and they'll not be able to leave off saying it.

SATURDAY MEN

They bet what they have on the red
of a Saturday night that would grant them
a better life that would cast to oblivion
the pile of chores they'd prefer not
to have to do at the end of a long day,
so they might worship weekends
so as to believe that reality
is not to be found between Monday and Friday.
Saturday they get up late and will buy
for the whole week, and meet up
to go out to supper, and in bars at night
talk about things that matter to them:
cars, football, money and women.
And they all end up in really dark basements
with bright lights, and smoke, and din.
They smoke and drink a lot, and talk loudly
into ears that don't want
to listen to them. And they show off by dancing,
until they are tired and go back to laying siege
to someone who seems to be paying them more attention,
a girl allured by the banter
they have managed to fabricate – though not enough
to persuade her to get into bed.
And they go back to smoking and drinking, and agitating
a body that is tired with so much night.

De cop s'atura tot, i per fi senten
tot el xarrabascat que els atabala
– el que abans les cançons emmascaraven –,
quan de fons els cambrers endrecen gots
i els cops són com les hores que han tocat,
igual que els últims salts que fa la bola
a la ruleta, i és prop d'aturar-se.
Deixen el frec humà, l'eixordadora
música, i surten cansats a aquest dia
que trenca però és encara fosc.
Quan arriben a casa van al vàter,
s'estiren sobre el llit amb la fatiga,
amb la pudor de fum que els fa la roba
i una aspra sensació de boca seca.
Ho han perdut tot. Acaba sortint negre.

LA CIUTAT PROHIBIDA

Després de tantes nits d'insomni i rates
que la desperten a mig son, enmig
del fosc, al seu costat. Després de tants
nervis a flor de pells per infeccions
d'orina, i menstruacions que arriben tard,
s'ha reservat l'ofici de topògraf
i cronista d'aquest nou món que és seu.
Recorda aquella nit que es van conèixer:
les músiques, les llums i les paraules
d'aquella gran conversa interminable
que encara van reprendre ahir a la nit.
Des de llavors no ha fet res més que viure
els seus moments i prendre'n una imatge
de la qual és fotògraf i assistent,
per poder-la ensenyar als seus coneguts,
com sempre es fa després d'unes vacances.
Però hi ha un món perdut que queda lluny,
allà on ella ha viscut tants i tants anys,
i que l'ha fet com és, i on ell no hi té
permís de residència, i no ha pogut
travessar les muralles ni el fossat.
Intueix les teulades i els jardins,
i els animals que hi ha pels crits que fan
les feres, i ell escolta amb atenció:

Suddenly everything stops, and at last they hear
all the din that stuns them –
the same din that earlier the songs were cloaked in –,
when at the back the waiters are stacking glasses
and the crashes are like the hours that have struck,
like the final leaps the ball makes
on the roulette wheel, and it's close to stopping.
They leave the human jostle, the deafening
music, and go out tired into that day
which is breaking but is still dark.
When they get home they go to the lavatory,
they stretch out on the bed with their weariness,
with the stink of smoke that their clothes exude
and the unpleasant feel of a dry mouth.
They have lost it all. The game ends up in the black.

THE FORBIDDEN CITY

After so many nights of insomnia and rats
waking her mid-dream, in the midst
of the darkness, beside her. After all those
nerves jangling along her skin due to urinary
infections, and periods coming late,
he has reserved for himself the task of topographer
and chronicler of this new world that is his.
He remembers the night they met:
the music, the lights and the words
of that long and interminable conversation
that they resumed once more last night.
Since then he has done nothing but live
these moments and extract from them an image
of which he is photographer and participant,
in order to show it to those he knows,
as you always do after the holidays.
But there is a lost world that remains far off,
where she has lived for years and years,
which has made her what she is, and where he has no
residential permit, and has been unable
to smash through the walls or cross the ditch.
He guesses at its roofs and gardens,
and the animals that are there from the cries
the wild beasts make, and he listens to them carefully:

suposa arquitectura i geografia,
però és un mal cartògraf del passat.
Ell ha explorat els set mars dels seus iris,
però mai no sabrà aquells ulls que feia
l'emperadriu a la ciutat prohibida.

ELS MALS LECTORS

Els grans se'ls miren des de dalt com juguen:
han trobat un gripau dins del jardí.
L'estiren de les potes i el contemplen,
però passat un primer instant de dubte,
de meravella en descobrir un volum
que no van creure mai que respirés,
el fan volar per l'aire, i cau d'esquena
mostrant un ventre blanc, tou i estriat.
Estabornit, s'intenta redreçar
i fugir del perill, però l'encalcen,
just quan els cau als peus la cigarreta
que des del balcó estant els han llençat
amb un crit que anuncia la tortura
que els pares van aprendre fa molts anys,
quan van rebentar-ne un amb un petard.
Han fet fumar el gripau, n'han disposat,
i han fet ensumar al gos la mansuetud
de la bèstia que amaga el seu mareig,
maldestrament, a sota d'unes fulles.
Si ara el disseccionessin panxa enlaire,
l'obrissin en canal sobre una taula,
veurien que l'aspecte repugnant
amaga un nou encert de la natura
que ha anat perfeccionant, amb milers d'anys,
per convertir-lo en déu, al mig del fang,
d'alguna bassa de mosquits d'estiu.
Amb tot, els nens, massa ignorants, el punxen,
el van girant amb un bastó trobat
que és símbol de l'enginy que hi ha als seus dits,
del desànim per no saber què fer-ne.
Els criden a sopar, s'acaba el joc,
i mentre aixequen més d'una protesta,
i obliden la joguina que han tingut,
el batraci s'allunya amb un pas lent,

he imagines architecture and geography,
but he is a poor cartographer of the past.
He has explored the seven seas of her eyes
but he will never know the expression she wore,
the empress of the forbidden city.

BAD READERS

The grown-ups look down on them where they are playing:
they have found a toad in the garden.
They pull it by its legs and stare at it,
but after a moment of doubt,
marvelling as they discover a bulk
they never believed could be breathing,
they make it fly through the air, and it falls sideways
revealing a white belly, soft and striped.
Stunned, it attempts to straighten itself
and escape from the danger, but they pursue it,
just when there falls at their feet the cigarette
thrown down to them from the jutting balcony
with a cry foretelling the torture
the parents learned many years ago,
when they blew one of them up with a firecracker.
They have made the toad smoke, they have made use of it,
and they have made the dog inhale the docility
of the creature that conceals its dizziness,
clumsily, beneath some leaves.
If they were now to dissect it, belly upwards,
if they were now to slit it open along its length on a table-top,
they would see that the repulsive aspect
hides one of the new triumphs of nature,
which over thousands of years has been being perfected
to turn it into a god, amid the mud,
of a pond of summer gnats.
In spite of this, the children, too ignorant, poke it,
dragging it in circles with a stick they have found,
which is a symbol of the knowledge at their finger-tips,
of their discouragement, not knowing what to do with it.
They are called in to supper, the game is over,
and while they raise more than one cry of protest,
and forget the toy they have been playing with,
the batrachian creeps slowly away,

imprecís, que arrossega un fat terrible.
Demà quan serà clar, i formigues negres
es vagin passejant sobre el seu ventre,
algun agró sabrà treure'n profit.

PER SELVES I DESERTS

"Love me with thine open youth
In its frank surrender;
With the vowing of thy mouth,
With its silence tender"
ELIZABETH BARRETT BROWNING

Si hagués tingut tan sols el que has tingut tu en mi,
algú més gran, vint anys entre tu i jo,
i un horitzó, distant i extens, just als teus peus.
Ets el patrici que heretarà aquest món.

A tu et va escaure tot, la gràcia i la bellesa,
la incòmoda imperícia que els nois teniu
t'ha estalviat un immortal que et vol coper,
i vius tendre i segur del teu present.

Jo hagués venut tants anys, que també ara he perdut,
per escapar d'aquell món de noiets:
teatre i òpera, sopars, concerts i recitals
i el blanc i el negre d'una actriu que ja és morta.

Les nits de discoteca van fer petar il·lusions
com gots llargs, líquid dolç que s'estavella,
i moltes nits, de llençols freds i carn que cou,
de mesos llargs que ja veiem com èpoques.

Aquest ha estat com mai l'únic hivern suau
que em serà donat viure, i mentre tu,
fill pròdig, vas tornant cap a casa amb les noies,
que et somien en nits de blancs llençols,

jo seguiré escapant descalça per nevades,
sense portal, per selves i deserts,
com la boja que, esperitada, fuig d'un passat
que la cerca amb l'estómac buit d'un llop.

unsteadily, trailing a sad fate.
Tomorrow when it's light, and black ants
go marching across its belly,
some heron will benefit from it.

THROUGH JUNGLES AND DESERTS

"Love me with thine open youth
In its frank surrender;
With the vowing of thy mouth,
With its silence tender"

ELIZABETH BARRETT BROWNING

If I had only had what you have had in me,
        someone older, twenty years between us,
and an horizon, stretching far and wide, just at your feet.
        You are the patrician who will inherit this world.

Everything fell into your lap, grace and beauty,
        the awkward lack of experience that you boys have
has saved you an immortal who wants you as cup-bearer,
        and you live tenderly and secure in your present.

I should have sold so many years that now I have also lost,
        so as to escape that world of little boys:
theatre and opera, dinners, concerts, recitals
        and the black and white of an actress who is now dead.

Nights at the discothèque have smashed illusions
        like tall tumblers, sugary drinks that shatter everywhere,
and many nights, with cold sheets and burning flesh,
        of long months that we now see as epochs.

This has been as never before the only mild winter
        given to me to live while you,
prodigal son, are coming back home with the girls,
        who were dreaming of you on nights of white sheets,

I shall continue to run away barefoot through snowstorms,
        with no doorways, through jungles and deserts,
like the crazy woman, possessed, running away from a past
        that pursues her with the empty stomach of a wolf.

PRINCIPI DE PLAER

Portrait d'Edward James, 1937

Què amaga la mà esquerra, la sinistra?
Per què amb la dreta toques el món sòlid,
la fusta material que et parapeta,
com l'urpa d'un ocell que no s'enfonsa
en el món pla, fet per les branques?
És tot tan fosc i inhòspit. Mig oculs,
l'or del botó de puny que et descobreix
i l'estil elegant del teu vestit
que delata qui ets en societat.
I tu, tot tu, fulgor de llum de l'èxit,
cremes de pur alcohol d'etern present:
la intensitat potent que els altres veuen,
que desitgen que siguis, vol ser teva,
i tu els retornes aquell món brillant
que havien somiat sentir-se propi,
i que la clara imatge del teu nom
– del seu passat, del teu futur – n'és mostra.
Tots volen ser la roca dura al fons
d'una sima engolada, o pedra d'or
de molts quirats que porta un riu convuls
corrent avall, sense cap dic.
                                    I som
els meteorits que una explosió estel·lar
va escopir a la galàxia i molts mil·lennis
han desgastat l'espai en pura pols,
i han caigut per atzar dins de la vida,
al marge d'un camí.
                          Aquí n'hi ha un.

TORTUGUES

Es feréstec i trist aquest so fosc:
les tortugues copulen al jardí.
S'escometen, i fugen, i s'atrapen,
intenten acoblar-se però els costa,
encara que la força dels seus gens,
un ímpetu ancestral que els bull endins,
desitja sobreviure-les, usar-les,
i els fa cremar la sang sota la closca.

THE PLEASURE PRINCIPLE
   Portrait of Edward James. 1937

What does the left hand, the sinister, conceal?
Why, with the right, do you touch the solid world,
the wooden material that protects you,
like the claw of a bird that doesn't sink into
the flat world, made by branches?
It's all so dark and inhospitable. Half-hidden,
the gold of a cuff-link that reveals you
and the elegant cut of your suit
that betrays your rank in society.
And you, the whole of you, the dazzling light of success,
you burn with the pure spirit of the eternal present:
the powerful intensity that others see,
that they want you to be, want to be yours,
and you give back to them that shining world
they had dreamed of experiencing as their own,
and of which the clear image of your name –
of their past, of your future – is the proof.
They all want to be the hard rock at the bottom
of an engulfed layer of basal crust, or gold-bearing stone
of many carats that a river in spate carries
downsteam, with no dam.
                              And we are
the meteorites which an explosion among the stars
has spat out into the galaxy and many millennia
have worn away space into pure dust,
and have fallen by chance into life,
at the side of a road.
                              Here is one of them.

TORTOISES

It's wild and sad, this dark sound:
the tortoises are mating out in the garden.
They rush at each other, and flee, and catch each other,
they try to couple but it's difficult,
even though the strength of their genes,
an ancestral impulse that boils inside them,
wishes to survive them, wear them out,
and makes their blood burn beneath the shell.

L'escut del ventre topa amb la cuirassa,
i no es miren ni es troben la carn rèptil.
Fa soroll el plaer que els porta al risc
de quedar panxa enlaire i no tombar-se,
quietes i sense alè, cuites pel sol;
que el principi vital que mou l'espècie
ja s'ha perpetuat en l'individu.
És feréstec i trist aquest so fosc,
com els crits i els gemecs que fa la nit.

CANÇÓ INFANTIL

Per què els nens ens demanen
que tornem a explicar
amb les paraules justes
els contes que escoltàvem?

Hi havia una vegada,
en un temps molt antic,
i en terra molt llunyana
un príncep coratjós
i una princesa maca.

Llops malèvols i bruixes,
porquets i rates sàvies,
amb dubtes i flaqueses,
amb estultícia humana.

Potser és tot una trama,
un ordre immemorial
que es repeteix sens falta,
i tots som els intèrprets
de quotidiana faula.

Repartits els papers,
coneguts de la infància,
improvisem guions
amb semblants personatges.

Reconèixer els caràcters,
fer del vital embull
una previsió exacta,

The shield of their belly bumps against armour-plating,
and they don't look at each other or encounter reptilian flesh.
Noise comes from the pleasure that brings the risk
of finding themselves belly-up and unable to right themselves,
motionless, without breath, burnt by the sun:
for the vital principle that impels the species
has already been perpetuated in the individual.
It's wild and sad, this dark sound,
like the cries and groans that night makes.

CHILDREN'S SONG

Why do children ask us
to tell them again
with the same words
the tales we used to listen to?

Once upon a time,
long, long ago,
in a far-off land
there was a brave prince
and a beautiful princess.

Malevolent wolves and witches,
piglets and wise rats,
with doubts and flaws,
wtih human stupidity.

Maybe it's all a plot,
an immemorial order
that unfailingly repeats itself,
and we are all the interpreters
of everyday fables.

With the parts all allocated
and known from infancy,
we improvise scripts
with similar characters.

Recognising the personas,
creating out of the lively muddle
an exact forecast,

deu ser font de plaer,
seguretat estable.

No hi caben variacions,
ni tipus nous a l'auca,
sense aixecar protesta
de l'atenta quitxalla.

Per tant, enllà del marge
no pot haver-hi vida
estranya als ulls dels altres,
i cal repetir els hàbits
i els actes esperables.

Un jo coherent i rar
desperta malfiança
en la creença eterna:
tot jo ha de ser un nosaltres.

CARN BEN ENDINS

Hi ha llocs on no podré tornar mai més,
indrets perduts on van portar-m'hi els pares:
el bosc de sabateres i toixons,
el peu de la nesplera amb punxes d'arç
amb fruits per ser guardats en bressol d'or.
I juntament, serrats arrodonits i estranys
que es drecen des de lluny al cor,
al nord estanys glacials d'isards, marmotes,
al sud les terres planes inundades
de curtes cintes verdes i palmeres,
i eixarreïdes planes i fruiters,
o els recs per buscar cuca per pescar,
i els farallons on recolzar les canyes…
Cartografia d'un país viscut,
perquè va ser dels mots dels meus, i alguns
ara el tornen concrets mapes a escala
d'un sòl lunar, quan és un lloc immens
                    carn ben endins.

must be a source of pleasure,
of stability and safety.

There's no room for variations,
or new types in the strip cartoons,
without raising protests
from the attentive crowd of kids.

And so, beyond the margin
there can be no life
that is foreign in the eyes of the rest,
and you have to repeat the habits
and actions they are waiting for.

A strange and coherent I
awakens mistrust
in the eternal belief:
every I must be an us.

DEEP IN THE FLESH

There are places I'll never be able to go back to,
long-lost haunts where my parents took me:
the wood with the boletus and the badgers,
the foot of the medlar all spiny with blackthorn,
with fruits to be kept in a golden cradle.
And together, strange and rounded peaks
that rise up from far away in the heart,
to the north, icy lakes with wild goats and marmots,
to the south, flat lands flooded
with small green strips and palm trees,
and parched plains and orchards,
or ditches where we'd look for bait to fish with,
and the pointed rocks on which to rest our rods...
Cartography of a land that has been lived,
because it was through my own folk's words,
and some now turn it to detailed maps, the scale
of a lunar land, when it's an enormous place
                    deep in the flesh.

PER TROBAR ARRELS

Ve d'un món, corromput amb mots estranys
per segles de domini i de veïnatge,
que el fang ha anat tacant o s'ha empassat.
És d'una terra on tenen nom les cases,
on s'hereten motius sense cognoms.
Recorda encara un temps de fred de ferro,
de molls cremant, ansats, i torrapans,
d'ensulfatar, lligar, d'anar a fer llenya,
d'aviram a les gàbies de l'eixida.
Coneix tots els pedaços i els sargits,
i unes cançons d'infant que ningú sap.
Ara és com l'estranger en un país nou
que ningú entén quan diu els mots dels seus,
com el mut que demana caritat,
i vol els sots, les coses que va perdre.
Senglar que furga inútilment en fang
        per trobar arrels.

COSINS GRANS

Escoltava Elvis Presley i fumava.
Tenia un joc de cartes grans i estranyes
que li servien per predir el futur
alt com sequoies des de sota –
per mi una multiplicació difícil
amb poc més d'una mà d'edat, llavors.

Em portava al seu cotxe groc, petit,
al cine, i repetia que trobava
que la Liza Minelli era guapíssima,
i jo li deia que ella era ho era més.

No crec que n'estigués enamorat
– ni amb aquell amor pur de nen, mimètic –,
però em va donar mà en un joc de grans:
enraonar amb una dona que t'estimes,
tastar el que se't prohibeix (begudes negres),
poder malgastar el temps quan es fa fosc.

LOOKING FOR ROOTS

He comes from a world corrupted with strange words
through centuries of domination and neighbourhood,
which mud has spattered or swallowed up.
He comes from a land where the houses have names,
where nicknames are inherited without surnames.
He still remembers a time cold as iron,
of burning fire-tongs, one-handled pots, toasting-forks,
of dusting with sulphate, tying up plants, going for kindling,
of poultry in caged runs in the back-yard.
He knows all the knacks of patching and darning clothes
and a handful of children's songs that no one else knows.
Now he is like the stranger in a new country
whom no one understands when he utters the words of his own people,
like the dumb man who begs for charity,
and wants empty hollows, the things he has lost.
Wild boar jabbing futilely at mud
          looking for roots.

OLDER COUSINS

She used to listen to Elvis Presley and she smoked.
She had a pack of large and strange cards
with which she'd predict the future
far-off as sequoias seen from below –
a difficult multiplication for me
counting my years on little more than one hand.

She drove me in her small yellow car
to the cinema, and said over and over she thought
that Liza Minelli was really beautiful,
and I told her that she was even more so.

I don't think I was really in love with her –
not with that pure, childish, mimetic love –
but she gave me a hand in a grown-up game:
chatting with a woman you really like,
tasting what's forbidden to you (dark-looking drinks),
being able to waste your time when it gets dark.

Va anar a viure a ciutat per treballar,
i un malentès d'aquells de les famílies
me la va separar per sempre més,
com un llamp sobre un arbre genealògic.

Hem coincidit a algun enterrament,
i ara ens trobem pel poble, al cap dels anys
(que han fet que s'assemblés a qui volia),
i no sabem què dir-nos, i parlem
de com ens van les coses, d'on anem,
i repartim records – com coneguts.

No he pogut recordar què va predir,
si aquesta nostra sort estava escrita,
però aquell que vaig ser mai no ha oblidat
dos dibuixos maldestres a les cartes:
l'ossuda mort
                          i l'arbre del penjat.

L'OCELL OCULT

Recordo de petit les orenetes
fent nius al voladís de la teulada:
no van tornar, i els caus de fang van caure.
Quan jugava, els pardals, en fila als fils,
estesos, resignaven el mal temps –
i a vegades també aquells núvols mòbils
d'estornells fent figures de cent ales.
Encara vénen a aplegar les granes
i es fonen, humilment, entre les garses
que salten pel jardí, cucotejant,
i fan sonar carraques a l'estiu.
Hem vist creuar uns quants ànecs, cap cigonya,
i voleien enllà gavines tipes.
De coloms no n'hi ha hagut, però un bon dia
van començar a criar un parell de tórtores:
han nascut dues notes amb perfídia
i enmig de les antenes molts més vols.
Quan el fosc ve o se'n va, si el fred s'espanta,
refilen rossinyols, discrets i frescos.
Amb els anys graten terra plomes brutes
amb bec esquerp i groc que n'han dit merles.

She went to live in town to work,
and one of those family misunderstandings
cut her off from me for ever,
like a flash of lightning striking a family tree.

We bumped into each other at some funeral,
and now we meet in the village, after all these years
(that have made her look like the one she wanted to),
and we don't know what to say to each other, and we talk
of how things are going, of where we're going,
and we share memories – like people who know each other.

I've not been able to remember what she predicted,
if this fate of ours was written,
but the one I was then has never forgotten
two clumsy drawings among the cards:
the big, bony, dead woman
                    and the tree of the hanged man.

THE HIDDEN BIRD

I remember when I was small the swallows
making their nests under the roof-eaves:
they never returned, and the mud shelters fell down.
While I played, sparrows, perched in long lines
on the wires, resigned themselves to the bad weather –
and sometimes too those moving clouds
of starlings making shapes from a hundred wings.
They still come to pick up seeds
and mingle, humbly, with the magpies
that hop around the garden, grubbing about,
their cries rattling harshly in the summer.
We have seen a few ducks passing over, but no storks,
and well-fed gulls flying in the distance.
There have been no pigeons at all, but one fine day
a pair of turtle-doves began to raise their young:
Two notes were born with obstinacy
and among the antennae many more flights.
When the darkness comes or goes, if the cold is fearful,
nightingales trill, fresh and discreet.
With the years, the dark feathers and shy, yellow beak
scratching the soil proclaimed the blackbirds' coming.

Ja ens hem acostumat als esgarips
que fa el paó, i als espinguets del gall.
Però d'un temps ençà canta un ocell
de timbre diferent i toc estrany,
que s'esquitlla, rabent, si el vull mirar.
No sé on és, no sé què és, però m'inquieta
desconèixer el seu nom, d'on ha nascut,
qui ha canviat el meu món perquè ara el senti,
per què ve sol i em fuig, i em canta a mi,
signe d'un moment buit, i aquest meu temps.

QUAN SIGUIS TRISTA

Contra W. B. Yeats

Quan siguis trista i grassa i ja no et mirin
els obrers en passar, i els pits et pengin,
i quan molt vella els néts no et reconeguin
el vesc dolç del teu cos, la pell de lliri

(que va atrapar tants homes, i una dona),
si els ensenyes les fotos, vora el foc,
no els parlis mai de mi, deixa'm a fora
del teu passat: furtiu d'un vedat clos.

No t'enyoris als llibres que vas viure
ni, pel que hauria estat, sentis cap pena:
ja no viuríem junts, no em parlaries,
ni hauries llegit mai aquest poema.

We have become accustomed to the shrieks
the peacock utters, and to the cock's crowing.
But for some time now a bird sings
with a different timbre and strange beat,
which hides itself, quickly, when I want to look at it.
I don't know where it is, I don't know what it is, but it bothers me
not to know its name, or where it was born,
or what has changed my world that I now hear it,
why it comes alone and flees from me, and sings to me,
sign of a hollow moment, and of this my time.

WHEN YOU ARE SAD

After W. B. Yeats

When you are sad and fat and workmen no longer
look at you as you pass, and your breasts droop,
and when you are ancient and the grandchildren fail
to recognise the sweet lure, the lily skin

(that caught so many men, and one woman),
when you show them the photos, beside the fire,
don't speak to them of me, leave me out
of your past: a poacher in a walled reserve.

Don't you be pining for the books you lived
or feel regret for all that might have been:
by then we'd no longer be together, you'd not
be speaking to me, nor ever have read this poem.

PHOTO: POL BARRÓS

PERE BALLART, born in Barcelona in 1964, is currently Professor of Literary Theory and Comparative Literature at the Autonomous University of Barcelona. Among his books of essays, many of them award-winning, are *Eironeia* (1994), a global study on the nature of literary irony, *El contorn del poema* (The Contour of the Poem, 1998), *El riure de la màscara* (Laughter in the Mask, 2007), *Obra vista* (Exposed Brickwork, 2009) and *La veu cantant* (The Singing Voice, 2011), all on the role of lyric poetry in modern and contemporary literature. He also has written regularly on current literary criticism for newspapers such as *El País* and *Avui*.

PHOTO: JEMIMAH KUHFELD

ANNA CROWE, born in Plymouth in 1945, is a poet and translator and the author of four poetry collections in English: *Figure in a Landscape* (2010), awarded the Callum MacDonald Memorial Award in 2011; *Skating Out of the House* (1997), *A Secret History of Rhubarb* (2006), *Punk with Dulcimer* (2006); one in Catalan / English bilingual edition: *L'ànima del teixidor* (2000); and one in Catalan: *Punk con salterio*, translated by Joan Margarit (2008). She has translated three of Joan Margarit's collections: *Tugs in the fog* (Bloodaxe, 2006, a Poetry Book Society Recommended Translation); *Barcelona, amor final* (2007, Catalan / Castilian / English trilingual edition); *Strangely happy* (Bloodaxe, 2011). She has also translated Anna Aguilar-Amat's *Música i escorbut* (Blesok, 2006), and, with Iolanda Pelegrí, an anthology of Catalan poetry, *Miralls d'aigua* (*Light Off Water*, Scottish Poetry Library / Carcanet Press, 2006). Along with several other writers, she was a founder member of StAnza, the Scottish international poetry festival, and was artistic director during its first seven years. She has twice won the Peterloo Open Poetry competition, and in 2005 won a travelling scholarship from the Society of Authors.

Other anthologies of poetry in translation published
in bilingual editions by Arc Publications include:

Altered State: An Anthology of New Polish Poetry
EDS. ROD MENGHAM, TADEUSZ PIÓRO, PIOTR SZYMOR
Translated by Rod Mengham, Tadeusz Pióro *et al*

A Fine Line: New Poetry from Eastern
& Central Europe
EDS. JEAN BOASE-BEIER, ALEXANDRA BÜCHLER, FIONA SAMPSON
Various translators

A Balkan Exchange:
Eight Poets from Bulgaria & Britain
ED. W. N. HERBERT

The Page and The Fire:
Poems by Russian Poets on Russian Poets
ED. PETER ORAM
Selected, translated and introduced by Peter Oram

Six Slovenian Poets
ED. BRANE MOZETIČ
Translated by Ana Jelnikar, Kelly Lennox Allen
& Stephen Watts, with an introduction by Aleš Debeljak
NO. 1 IN THE 'NEW VOICES FROM EUROPE & BEYOND' ANTHOLOGY SERIES,
SERIES EDITOR: ALEXANDRA BÜCHLER

Six Basque Poets
ED. MARI JOSE OLAZIREGI
Translated by Amaia Gabantxo,
with an introduction by Mari Jose Olaziregi
NO. 2 IN THE 'NEW VOICES FROM EUROPE & BEYOND' ANTHOLOGY SERIES,
SERIES EDITOR: ALEXANDRA BÜCHLER

Six Czech Poets
ED. ALEXANDRA BÜCHLER
Translated by Alexandra Büchler, Justin Quinn
& James Naughton, with an introduction by Alexandra Büchler
NO. 3 IN THE 'NEW VOICES FROM EUROPE & BEYOND' ANTHOLOGY SERIES,
SERIES EDITOR: ALEXANDRA BÜCHLER

Six Lithuanian Poets
ED. EUGENIJUS ALIŠANKA
Various translators, with an introduction by Eugenijus Ališanka
NO. 4 IN THE 'NEW VOICES FROM EUROPE & BEYOND' ANTHOLOGY SERIES,
SERIES EDITOR: ALEXANDRA BÜCHLER

Six Polish Poets
ED. JACEK DEHNEL
Various translators, with an introduction by Jacek Dehnel
NO. 5 IN THE 'NEW VOICES FROM EUROPE & BEYOND' ANTHOLOGY SERIES,
SERIES EDITOR: ALEXANDRA BÜCHLER

Six Slovak Poets
ED. IGOR HOCHEL
Translated by John Minahane, with an introduction by Igor Hochel
NO. 6 IN THE 'NEW VOICES FROM EUROPE & BEYOND' ANTHOLOGY SERIES,
SERIES EDITOR: ALEXANDRA BÜCHLER

Six Macedonian Poets
ED. IGOR ISAKOVSKI
Various translators, with an introduction by Ana Martinoska
NO. 7 IN THE 'NEW VOICES FROM EUROPE & BEYOND' ANTHOLOGY SERIES,
SERIES EDITOR: ALEXANDRA BÜCHLER

Six Latvian Poets
ED. IEVA LEŠINSKA
Translated by Ieva Lešinska, with an introduction by
Juris Kronbergs
NO. 8 IN THE 'NEW VOICES FROM EUROPE & BEYOND' ANTHOLOGY SERIES,
SERIES EDITOR: ALEXANDRA BÜCHLER